ISLINGTON

KU-288-619

...*em* on or before the last date stamped below or you may
To renew an item call the number below, or
gov.uk/libraries. You will need

Jill Soloway is the Emmy and Golden Globe Award-winning creator of *Transparent*. Previously a writer and executive producer for *Six Feet Under*, *How to Make It in America*, and *United States of Tara*, Jill's first feature film, *Afternoon Delight*, won the 2013 Directing Award at Sundance. They also co-created and directed the Amazon series *I Love Dick*. Jill lives in Los Angeles.

ISLINGTON LIBRARIES

3 0120 02799478 9

"This is a story about self-doubt, self-discovery, and the triumph of self-actualization. It is imperative reading for anyone who wants to gain a better understanding of what it means to be Other in this world—what it means to discover who you are, to understand that each of us deserves happiness, and gathering the grit to go after it. I could not put this hilarious and heartfelt book down."

—CHELSEA HANDLER

"Jill Soloway's extraordinary memoir, *She Wants It,* is a compendium of the heart, a brave piece of literature that pulses from the page with its unique journey through the grace and guts of living honestly and intentionally in a world that often aims to deny us of both. Jill's story is both an illumination and an education, one that broke me as a reader, then put me back together again, wholly changed and forever redefined."

—AMBER TAMBLYN

"Jill Soloway is not only a stunningly talented series creator, they're an archangel, here to rid us of the patriarchy. It's a grand mission and it's not easy going, *She Wants It* is their wild-winged, softhearted share-all. I loved their book so much—it is about everything I'm interested in; a personal life amidst daring creative endeavors."

—JANE CAMPION

"If anyone has led a more wildly interesting life and written about it more brilliantly than Jill Soloway, this devourer of such hasn't found it. Grab on and grab hold! You'll be laughing and crying the whole way through."

—NORMAN LEAR

"Pages are just another canvass that Jill uses to share their truth and artistry. *She Wants It* gives a timely front-row seat to gender exploration and storytelling that entertains as it inspires."

—SARAH KATE ELLIS

"Fierce, funny, and fabulous—this book is a triumph!"

—MARGARET CHO

"*She Wants It* reads like the memoir you've always dreamed of writing, if only you were as talented and funny and altogether endearing as Jill Soloway. The book's casual and effortless-seeming prose belies the seriousness of Soloway's intentions until the moment when you realize that you are reading a thrilling meditation on everything important, from the way women traditionally inhabit the world to the new paradigms of power and gender that they are claiming as their own. It will make you question many of your assumptions—or, perhaps, clutch ever more tightly to them—but, either way, you will read it with rapt interest and feel like your horizons have broadened when you're done. Jill Soloway is still the smartest kid in the class, coaxing us all along with them on their profound and daring journey of self-discovery."

—DAPHNE MERKIN

"*She Wants It* is an extraordinary examination of feminism, ambition, artistic desire, chance, and career by one of the greatest American writer/directors working today. Soloway surveys the trajectory of their life and the creation of their groundbreaking series, *Transparent,* with courage, self-knowledge, humility, and wit. Their voice got inside me, I was totally hooked."

—CHRIS KRAUS

"In a world where gender doesn't mean what it used to, *She Wants It* offers so much more than a backstage peek into the autobiographical origins of *Transparent*. Jill Soloway's on a quest to figure out feminism for the twenty-first century—and wants you to want that, too."

—SUSAN STRYKER

"Jill Soloway's is one of our culture's most innovative minds, and *She Wants It* is a keen demonstration of the depth of their insight. As Soloway depicts their intertwined desire to create art with the need to be their complete self, in the face of a culture that seeks to limit them because of their gender, they do so with that ineffable combination of intellect, unpredictability, and wit that has made their films and TV shows so undeniably brilliant. *She Wants It* is a necessary read for anyone who has ever wrestled with desire, both as an artist and a human being."

—MEREDITH TALUSAN

"Jill Soloway is a very lucky queer. They get every break, and then help people who never get a break. They stumble at intimacy and then soar to new heights of connection and

self-knowledge. Jill takes Hollywood to the thorniest questions Hollywood didn't know existed. This is a rollicking
tale of how an enmeshed family sometimes brings out the
best."

—SARAH SCHULMAN

"Jill has a brilliant ability to communicate their creative
process. The nuts and bolts of bringing a story to fruition,
from life, thought, and inspiration to the screen and vice
versa. They're fearless about expressing their desires—for
creative control, for power, for equality, dammit—with no
apologies."

—SUSIE BRIGHT

Also by Jill Soloway

Tiny Ladies in Shiny Pants

SHE WANTS IT

DESIRE, POWER AND
TOPPLING THE PATRIARCHY

JILL SOLOWAY

1 3 5 7 9 10 8 6 4 2

Ebury Press, an imprint of Ebury Publishing
20 Vauxhall Bridge Road
London SW1V 2SA

Ebury Press is part of the Penguin Random House Group
of companies whose addresses can be found
at global.penguinrandomhouse.com

Penguin
Random House
UK

Copyright © Soloway Books, Inc., 2018

Soloway Books, Inc., have asserted their right to be identified
as the author of this work in accordance with the Copyright,
Designs and Patents Act 1988

Grateful acknowledgement is made to the following for
permission to reprint previously published material:
Page 120: Excerpt from *evolution*, copyright © 2018
by Eileen Myles.
Used by permission of Grove/Atlantic, Inc. Any third-party
use of this material, outside of this publication, is prohibited.

First published by Ebury Press in 2018
This edition published in 2019

www.penguin.co.uk

A CIP catalogue record for this book is available
from the British Library

ISBN 9781785032851

Printed and bound in Great Britain by Clays Ltd, Elcograf S.p.A.

MIX
Paper from
responsible sources
FSC® C018179

Penguin Random House is committed to a
sustainable future for our business, our readers
and our planet. This book is made from
Forest Stewardship Council® certified paper.

For Ellen

Author's Note

AS WITH MOST BOOKS, some names and dates have been changed to make friends more comfortable and to make the flow more flowing. I've also found it most helpful to stay loose with the pronouns. A few of us have been multiple genders over the course of this work. I boldly use the gender most suited to what I experienced at the time, and sometimes use the word "they" to name a gender that has shifted over the years. Sometimes when I use the word "Dad" I also use the word "she." I understand this is complex and sometimes uncomfortable; it is this discomfort that I hope will guide us into our nonbinary future. I am grateful for your trust.

Contents

1. ARE YOU SITTING DOWN?   1

2. LOOKING   17

3. CLIMBING   32

4. MOUNTAINTOPS   45

5. TAKING HER OUT FOR A SPIN   59

6. RUN RUN RUN   72

7. BEAT CHANGE   94

8. CRACKING OPEN   106

9. MAKING HISTORY   120

10. WE'RE NOT ALLOWED TO WANT   136

11. YOU GOT WHAT YOU WANTED   154

12. GO TOWARD IT   173

13. I AM / I WANT   185

14. OH, FUCK   208

15. THE VULNERABLE FUTURE   223

Acknowledgments   239

ARE YOU SITTING DOWN?

BEFORE THE PHONE CALL, IT WAS AN ORDINARY SUNDAY. I WAS SIT-ting at the kitchen table with my youngest son, Felix. It was one of those bleary-eyed mornings when you wonder when you will ever be able to sleep until ten again.

The answer, by the way, is never. Okay, fine, when they're eight they can get themselves up, pour their own cereal, watch cartoons on their own, and you can sleep. Except you can't, because you're half-awake in a shame spiral about what a shitty mom you are because you're letting your kid watch so much TV. Again.

Getting old is this: you have a kid or two, and now you never sleep, you only ever get an imitation of sleep, something sleep-like, and this ages you. That's why people who live in nursing homes have thin hair and sad eyes instead of thick hair and bright eyes like the young people who get enough sleep. This lack of sleep will leave you with a depleted immune system, and when your kid goes to preschool they will bring home a million diseases and you will get sick, and then you will keep getting sick. Then one day you will realize that you have been sick for six weeks and then six months, and that the feeling that used to feel like a "light cold" is now just what it feels like to be alive. This will keep happening until you are old, actually old, and then you will die.

Even though my son Felix was only three years old on this particular Sunday morning, I knew the age that kids turn self-sufficient because I have an older son named Isaac who was in high school. When Isaac was twelve, I'd been silly enough to do it all over again, to get married and then pregnant and jump back into this utter foolishness. At the tender age of Oh Hell No, I'd reset the clock to zero and had a baby at a time when some rural folk become grammaws. It was on this morning, when I was really feeling my grammaw age, that Felix had come schluffling into our room at the crack of dawn. I poked at Bruce, begging.

Hun? Hun? Hun?

I got to bed late last night, honey; can it be your turn this morning?

You get to bed late every night, honey, but okay, fine, I'M UP I'M UP I'M UP here we go—wait, don't turn on that light—it hurts Mommy's eyes—yes, I've got blankie and husky dog—

Felix and I went downstairs. I put on *Dora* and hid under a blanket and tried to sleep. But my brain was already *buzzbuzzbuzz* so we went to the kitchen, and I did what I'd learned years before with Isaac to pass the hours between five and eight A.M., when time moves at one-quarter speed: I poured a bowl of Honey Nut Cheerios and we rolled calls on speakerphone. I started on the East Coast because the hour would be only vaguely ungodly there.

I expected my sister, Faith, to be up. Faith has a daughter, and sometimes over double FaceTime and double cereal we let the kids have at it while we flatten into a joyful, unconscious state of being. When Faith and I are in the same room—or even the same Skype window—we are in heaven, instantly freed of obligations. Our jaws unhinge and all filters lift; we stop watching closely and recording slights like we do with the rest of the world. We go back to our original sister selves—that is, one-half of the perfect circle of love we invented together when we were kids.

In our childhood home, Faith and I were the only happy couple in sight. Our parents zoomed off into their own tunnels of distraction. My mom's tunnel was the civil rights movement and my dad's tunnel was a melancholy one: he was a workaholic anesthesiologist who later became a workaholic psychiatrist. This gave Faith and me plenty of time to lie on the floor on our tummies, doodling on our parents' vinyl copies of the cast recordings of *Hair* and *Jesus Christ Superstar*, and improvising inappropriate songs on the piano. We invented worlds and sometimes plays that we shared with other kids, but mostly we were the protagonists, *Faith and Jill Superstar*, and we were happy, laughing and in love with each other. Our two puzzle pieces made up one complete person. While our parents slept back to back with miles between them, Faith and I spooned sweatily for ten hours a night. There was a moment when our mom moved us into separate rooms (at our request), but on night two, Faith raced down the hallway and back to my bed.

When Faith and I got bored with each other inside the house, which was almost never, we ventured outside to organize the neighborhood children into semi-professional, wildly successful theatrical productions. Faith and I and a gaggle of other kids in dirty fur-lined-hooded jackets mounted our own version of *The Wizard of Oz* with tickets for five cents for the neighbors and pizza parties afterward that felt like East Village nights out, except we were eight.

Faith and I had a short, yearlong rough patch during high school when she was a band nerd and I was into lip gloss, but soon after we snapped back into best-friend formation and shared a mind. After college we moved into an apartment on the Gold Coast in Chicago with our best friend, Robin. It was a two-bedroom so we let Robin have the single room and Faith and I shared. Yes, as adults we still enjoyed sharing a bedroom. At least we had two single beds.

During that time in Chicago we dated each other pretty much exclusively. We would go to the sets at Second City, which were after-show free improv sessions where our community was all of the soon-to-be-famous men.

We started a theater company and put on plays with our gangs of compatriot creatives. It was just like when we were little, except that *People* magazine would write about us occasionally. The taste of fame pulled us west, and in our early twenties, we moved to L.A. and broke into show business as the Soloway Sisters.

One day, Faith fell in love with someone other than me; she came out as a lesbian and declared her love to a woman named Harlie. I stayed a straightbian and tilted toward artsiness and weed. Faith escaped to Boston, where she became a teacher, anti-bullying expert, and folk music heroine. We longed for each other mightily but somehow understood that our love was too strong to allow for either one of us to have real relationships with anyone else, and that it was probably best that we live in separate cities. We still shared a conjoined psycho-spiritual system, where we found ourselves changing in tandem ways throughout our life.

But on this particular Sunday morning, Faith wasn't answering the phone. Felix and I tried Grandma next, but she must have been out and about. She still lives in Chicago and wakes up to write as early as four-thirty or five. My mom has published a number of books and has a blog presence, as well as a knack for going through my social media feeds trolling for her own fans. IF YOU LIKE JILL SOLOWAY, YOU'LL LOVE ELAINE SOLOWAY! is written on an imaginary sandwich board my mother wears around town. As annoying as it is to hear a woman who just turned eighty announcing her number of "likes" when we're waiting in line to see a movie, I believe that it is her unstoppable need for attention synthesized into an astonishingly propulsive ambition that is my greatest inheritance.

When we were growing up, my mom was the press aide for Mayor Jane Byrne and the director of communications for the superintendent of Chicago Public Schools. Our dining room table was never a dining room table; it was always a desk with stacks of cute mod wire inboxes, meticulously organized stationery, and a red IBM Selectric typewriter. Its *click-clacking* was the hot beating heart of our house. My mom was the editor of a newsletter for our neighborhood. Our neighborhood was a developer's dream about integration, a New Town called South Commons. New Towns were planned cities meant to redistribute people of color from crowded inner cities and white people from the suburbs into one mid-century modern Utopian life. Revolution was everywhere, the ERA and the Black Panthers, Jewish folks and black folks linking arms.

My mom's newsletter was called the *Commons Commentary*. She stitched it together with her tiny hands and rubber cement that you could roll into little brown balls while you watched her work. With rub-on transfer sheets of letters that you burnished onto the page, she described our world to itself. In it was a brilliant little comedic column she wrote called "Adam's Rib," which was a cross between Erma Bombeck and Joan Didion. Once a week, Faith and I dragged a red wagon filled with her newsletters and went door-to-door.

My mom had evolved over the years into a pretty tough-ass little grandma. She even has a tattoo. Like any good Jewish mom, it's of her kids' names. Sadly, the biker heart on her bicep that says Faith across the top and Jill across the bottom often gets her mistaken for a Faith Hill superfan.

Since Elaine was already out and about, we were left with Grandpa. He was usually home at that hour, not exactly the "getting out" type. Grandpa Harry also lived in Chicago and was saddled with a pervasive melancholy not uncommon among Jewish men of his generation. The kind of guy who, if it started to lightly drizzle outside, would raise both arms to the sky like Tevye and cry out, "Why me?!"

Growing up, I'd had a hard time understanding my dad, and a harder time getting along with him. When Faith and I were kids, he was either hiding out, depressed, or working. We spent most of our lives swerving out of his lane to let him pass. I remember his long working hours, getting home grumpy, the drawn curtains, the *Don't wake your father,* the *Oh shit, I think you woke your father,* rages followed by tearful apologies.

After Faith and I left home, he and my mom got divorced. She let him go, and it was easy enough for us to let him go, too, because this is what we had always done. Faith and I got chosen for Mom's team, supplying all of her lovey-dovey needs. Our dad skipped his turn to pick.

When they were married, my mom never said, "Honey, you seem wildly depressed and in a bubble." She never said, "Hey, babe, come out of your room and be with us." She just gathered up me and my sister and put on *Mary Tyler Moore* and *Rhoda* and *Phyllis* and made popcorn.

Over the years, Dad and I were mostly distant but had recently found our way into an easygoing détente of benign weather talk. It was in that spirit that Felix and I dialed. I put the phone on speaker, like I always do. Felix ate his cereal, and my dad, the six-foot-tall Jewish bear, said, "Hi, Jilly," just like he always did.

We talked for a few minutes, and then I asked how his weekend went. My dad said he had gone to a holiday party, and I asked, "Whose party?"

He said, "Do you really want to know?"

And I said, "Of course."

And he said: "Jilly? Are you sitting down?"

I realized that if I needed to be sitting down that I should probably turn off speakerphone so Felix wouldn't hear. Both of my parents could be counted on to casually blurt out a report of a shotgun-to-the-head death of someone on the news, a local kidnapping or Amber Alert, or the description of a bowel movement. "Kids in the room!" I have to say.

"Are you sitting down?" means something fucked up is coming.

I looked at Felix, snatched the phone off the table, clicked off the speaker, and held it to my ear.

"Jilly?" my dad said. "I'm coming out to you. I'm trans."

HIS VOICE WAS gentle. *Wait, did I hear that right?* My chest opened then caved. Rocket launch, then fast hollow quiet.

"Um, Dad, I love you, um, could ya—could ya—hold on one second?" I marshaled Felix to the TV room, put on *Dinosaur Train,* raced back to the kitchen table, and sat down, face-palming and sweating as I took in everything.

My dad started by telling me about a group called Chi Chapter that he'd been part of for years, a support group that sometimes had conferences. I googled it as we spoke; maybe the Internet could help me understand. I encountered a website with strong Angelfire vibes, *Victor/Victoria* clip art graphics, and descriptions of daylong boat events called FantaSea. I looked for sense in the images. Looked for signs of my father there.

He told me about a Hyatt in the Chicago suburbs where the girls (*what girls?*) would get rooms, change into femme clothes, then head to the restaurant for Caesar salads and Chardonnay. All of these people did this in secret, most were married and straight, and I wasn't really getting it. Married and straight men dressing up? He gabbed on excitedly while I dropped in and out, listening and googling and spinning. There was a nice woman at Nordstrom, he said, who had been helping him pick outfits for years. Nordstrom? Did I remember him going to Nordstrom? But now he was on to another story, this one about his friend Kim, who had ended up in jail, charged with prostitution, just for driving home from an event dressed en femme. *Jail?*

That morning I thought my dad was telling me about his odd hobby, but now I know that he was introducing me to a woman who had been living in our house my entire childhood. I had the wrong pronouns then and have only some of the right pronouns now but will use the wrong ones so you can see how wrong I had it.

I had been so in the dark that I thought my dad was joking.

Even though my brain was trying to jump out of my skull through the back of my neck, I knew to listen and be present, to speak with reassuring words: "I hope you know that I love you forever unconditionally, and I will always love you."

There was also some part of me that knew I would be making this into something. The feeling was undeniable. Not simply that this *could* be a movie or a show or a something, but that it *would* be a movie or a show or a something. An artistic knowing cracked through everything that had come before. This was part of my story, and I was going to tell it.

I took some deep breaths.

"Do you have a new name?" I asked.

"Carrie," she said. "Carrie London."

"Why a new last name?" I asked.

"Carrie London because, you know, I'm English."

"Of course," I said.

I had one more question.

"What about Mom and Faith?" I asked. "Do they know?"

"No. And please don't tell them. Let me do it."

Don't tell my mother or my sister? The thought was absurd. Not possible. My mom and my sister and I still comprised one three-headed triangle-shaped entity.

I texted Faith an urgent message:

—call Dad

—why?

—just do it and then call me after

—I can't I'm at the arboretum

—well as soon as you get home call him and then
  as soon as you hang up call me

—is everything okay?

—yes just do as I say

After my dad and I hung up, I ran upstairs. Bruce was sound asleep in Felix's bed. As part of our normal weekend morning migration, as soon as Felix came to our room, whoever got to go back to sleep would sleepwalk to Felix's bed.

Bruce had been flat-out mouth breathing since six A.M. I ran at him, pushed him awake, GET UP GET UP GET UP, then did an OH MY GOD dance and flapped my hands as I tried to tell him what I'd just heard.

"My dad is—my dad is—okay, so my dad just said he's—well—I think he meant he—um, sometimes wears women's clothing."

"Wait, what?" Bruce stayed under the covers.

"He said he's trans," I said.

"Is he getting a sex change operation?"

"No, it's not about surgery—I guess it's similar to crossdressing, which is different than transsexual, I mean, he said he's part of a group . . ."

A long silence, then:

"Does your mom know?" Bruce asked.

"No."

"Does Faith know?"

"She's calling him now."

"Holy fuck." Bruce finally got out of bed. I was hiding near the corner of the room. He tried to collect me in his arms, but neither of us was sure if I needed comforting. What had just happened? We both paced around the room for a second. I opened Felix's blinds. Looked at the marine-layer morning melancholy of downtown L.A.

"Where's Felix?"

"Watching TV."

"Where's Isaac?"

"Still sleeping. But I'm not going to tell him. We need to take some time, right?"

"Of course."

"Because I don't even know what this is yet," I said.

I KNEW THAT Isaac would be awake soon. I'd met Isaac's dad, Johnny, just before I turned thirty. He had a flop of long blond hair across one eye and a beautiful juicy face and full lips and he was a painter. He was an outlier in his family, a Palm Springs clan who had built the first gas stations and theaters out in the desert. He was totally irresponsible and I loved it. In those days I picked men for their ability to upend the very idea of dependable men. Proving something to myself. Together we were both wild and unmoored, and then somehow, one day, the idea of having a kid seemed adventurous and right to us. I had a strong feeling that maybe I would never find unconditional love, but if I had a kid then, okay, I would have at least one person.

The day Isaac was born, I sat in a rocker in my room at Cedars-Sinai, nursing him, and the world finally felt right. It was instantaneous, I was done. Cooked. My eyes and his eyes formed a circuit and we stayed that way, even till today, so much so that up until recently his therapist needed to say "enmeshed" about a hundred times before I could bear to entertain the notion.

When Isaac was three, Johnny moved out, and I officially became a single mother. I dated more men chosen for their ability to incinerate dreams of romantic stability. I saw families as cruel propaganda for something that I would not be involved in, no sir.

As Isaac grew up, we fell into a brother-sister thing, jumping in the car on Saturdays with a duffel bag and bathing suits to see where the day took us. We'd sneak into hotel pools or take the city bus and get off anywhere. Once we went to New York on short notice to walk around Central Park and randomly saw Gnarls Barkley playing live. It was summer and we were all singing "Crazy."

One Friday night when Isaac was eight, I was experimenting with throwing casual Shabbat dinners. The French doors were open, and at some point Bruce walked in. He was looking for his friend Jonah, who lived across the street and was one of my dinner guests. Bruce was wearing a white belt with pink-and-green Louis Vuitton symbols and white Nikes with pink-and-green swooshes, a just-gay-enough flair with his shaved head and gymnast posture. He was a photographer and had just come home from a yearlong surfing-the-world trip. We all enjoyed a great roast chicken meal and decided that after dinner we'd troop en masse to Scoops for brown bread ice cream. Afterward, though, everyone had somewhere else to be. Jessica's roommate needed her to come assess closet paint swatches. Jonah had to go home to his wife and daughter. Out of nine or ten people, the only ones left needing brown bread ice cream were us.

Bruce, Isaac, and me.

My car was in the shop and I had a rental that week, a big dumb Escalade, and I didn't feel like driving such a gigantic car, so as we headed outside and walked toward it, I said, "Ugh, I happen to have this huge-ass monster thing, you wanna drive it?"

Bruce said, "Sure I can. I drive a truck."

I looked up the street and saw his pickup parked behind my rental car. A Jewish man with a hot pink and acid green belt *and* a pickup truck. Hmm. Funny *and* smart *and* a surfer. Usually you had to pick between athletic success or the Ashkenazi genius gene.

There was a thunderclap and lightning strike as I tossed Bruce the keys, a midair flash of trust. He caught the keys.

We got in the Escalade. Closed the doors. A floating feeling rose inside the car, a new pressure system. Me in the passenger seat. Bruce in the driver's seat. Isaac in the back. We went to Scoops, and he knew exactly where to park, in the secret lot behind the bar across the street, and we all ordered ice cream. We ate our cones sitting in a triangle next to the little bay window.

Ah. This. The three of us.

We drove back to my house and Isaac and I got out of the car. Bruce gave me back the keys. We said goodbye and hugged awkwardly. I had just experienced this calm, completed feeling of being a family for half an hour with a total stranger. What kind of hug does that justice?

So, uh—bye.

Bye.

He drove away. Isaac and I walked up the steps.

Isaac looked at me and said, "Bruce! It's Bruce! We love Bruce!" I took him upstairs and tucked him in. Right before he fell asleep, he murmured, "Mommy, tonight I love you more than I've ever loved you in my life."

The next morning, I emailed Jonah: "Bruce Gilbert: gay or straight?"

Jonah wrote back: "Straight, and notoriously good in bed."

I laughed.

Bruce and I stayed in touch through text and email while he went on another surfing trip. When he got back, I invited him to a dinner party. It happened to be his birthday. He came over early. While I cooked, Bruce looked at the thousands of songs on my hard drive and made a playlist of ten, none of which I'd ever heard before.

I said, "Where did this music come from?"

"This is your music."

I was putting flowers in a vase while Jeff Tweedy sang "She's a Jar," about a girl who was *a sleepy kisser whose daddy's payday was not enough,* and I started crying.

A few months later Bruce moved in.

It immediately felt real, or real enough, and I started to dream: *Maybe we could be a real family; maybe Isaac could finally have a sibling.* But I was forty-two so I went to the doctor and he told me I was in menopause and that we would need an egg donor. We decided maybe one day we would get an egg donor, or adopt, or just forget about it and put all our energy toward parenting Isaac. We threw caution to the wind and had sex standing up in a cabin at a glamping resort during a family retreat a few moments before a game of Capture the Flag was about to start.

When I didn't get my period for a few months I thought I was indeed in menopause. After I felt nauseated for a couple days, I decided I should take a pregnancy test. I went to the drugstore and got one and peed on the stick and there it was.

We went to the obstetrician and she let us listen to the heartbeat, but then immediately told us there was a 10 percent chance our kid would have Down syndrome because of my elderly-ness. A month after that we had the amnio that finally told us we could relax—we were going to have a healthy baby boy.

I think it was right around this moment—when we were told we could finally breathe—that Bruce began wandering around nauseated, wondering what he had done. When we met, he had been trying to slide back into the music business in L.A. without too much chafing after his yearlong surfing trip. He still surfed often, and took beautiful photos, and played drums with his friends. He carried around a miniature Mason jar filled with weed, and he was the cutest dancer. I called him Sparkle Pony.

I started telling Bruce that he'd better propose soon. Friends harangued me, saying things like "men need to be tricked into proposing" and "men don't actually want to be married until they see their baby" and "men" this and "women" that and all kinds of things that made me think it was okay to not be on the same page about things like marriage and babies.

Ultimately, Bruce did propose. But he didn't want to have a wedding. We got our marriage license at the Beverly Hills Courthouse. Afterward we went over to his therapist's house.

Her name was Nancy and she was a hippie and had a brick labyrinth in her backyard. We walked the circular pattern of it until we landed in the middle. She read a poem aloud.

It had been four years since our wee little private wedding. We were both Isaac's parents now, and we had Felix as well. We were the picture of the good Jewish family even if we didn't always feel it. As far as I could tell, our relationship was just as alternately good and sucky as everyone else's.

AFTER THE CALL from my dad, I stood in the corner of the bedroom and stared at Bruce and Bruce stared at me and we knew something big had changed. I paced, trying to figure out what to do. Who to call. Did Faith know by now? What about my mom? Everything would get more real once they knew.

"So I should just go downstairs and act normal?" This is what we do, right, get on with our Sunday? Is this what a parent is, one face for your kids, to hide your inside face from them?

"Of course," Bruce said. "I'll be down in a minute."

I went downstairs to check on Felix. He was fine. I texted my therapist.

—Can you talk later?

When Bruce finally came downstairs he was wearing a dress from my closet. He didn't say anything, just acted all natural and talked about whether or not we were going to the farmers' market. I looked up. Saw him like that. We cracked up. Jesus fucking Christ.

2 LOOKING

THE NEXT DAY I WENT TO SEE MY THERAPIST. SHE IS KNOWN TO ME as The Great Ellen Silverstein (she doesn't go by that name). I'd found her back when Johnny and I were falling apart and I was taking on single motherhood and wondering how I'd gotten everything so wrong.

I parked outside of her office building on Lasky in Beverly Hills and walked in. My stomach cramped, just like it did back in high school when things were bad. I went into her outer office and pressed the light-up button. Sat in the leather chair. Stared at the mirrored closet where I always imagined she was secretly watching me through two-way glass. Scrutinized the fake Zen rock fountain with the wood bridge. Little burbling noises meant to muffle other clients.

Finally she opened the door, wide eyed. We hugged. I sat down. I loved the familiarity of her office. Warm beiges and caramel leather like something Paul Mazursky's production designer might dream up. Schefflera, ferns, and Venetian blinds.

I told her everything.

We both took a breath.

"Does this mean I need to start all over?" I asked.

"Of course not," she said.

I thought about all the days I'd sat in Ellen's office and whined: "But seriously, what is *wrong* with me?" She'd assure me that it was nothing, that I was perfectly perfect and perfectly normal, that *everyone* in the world shared the feeling of being Other.

She had always used the metaphor of a fun house mirror to describe how we make sense of our families of origin. For a decade, she'd been shepherding me away from my weird, wobbly, wide-hipped, tiny-headed freak reflections into a brand-new way of seeing myself, clear as Baccarat crystal. Much like reaching the upper levels of Scientology, our assumption was that this would take decades and decades of every Thursday at 12:40 P.M. to get there. I'd been searching so long that I'd started to suspect I'd forgotten just what it was that I was searching for.

It was time to put the pieces together.

My sister and I were raised upper middle class on the Near North Side of the city, where we'd moved after South Commons. I'd had a charge account at the local drugstore for candy and lotion. In terms of the basic needs of food, shelter, and central air, we were set. My mom was obsessed with me, and my dad suffered from depression and anxiety —which were called *blue moods* back then—but there was no alcoholism, no beatings, no gambling. We forgave my dad because we understood that he came by his deep melancholy honestly. He was raised in London by Grandpa Morris and Grandma Bella, and he had been terrified and little during the Blitz. On the rare occasion that he shared scraps of memories with us, he told us about being in the bomb shelter alone, mortally terrified, six years old and knowing

Hitler wanted to kill him. His dad's sister Eva was killed instantly when Hitler "dropped a bomb on her."

My mom's childhood was informed by a series of ways in which children might die. Tales of cousins running from the Holocaust. Then a serial killer who murdered a girl in her neighborhood and left parts of her chopped-up body in the sewer system. She'd told me she was always scared. But I didn't think we were any different from every other Jewish family in our world, except for a restlessness. My mom had a voracious appetite for political activism and liked to move every few years.

She gave Faith and me short boy-haircuts. We worshipped *Free to Be . . . You and Me*. I marched around proud, my eight-year-old tummy sticking out, convex. An orthopedist told my parents that they needed to put a brace on my leg so that my knee wouldn't end up turned in. My parents were afraid the brace would traumatize me, so I didn't get one. In elementary school, I was gobsmacked at the sheer number of male presidents along the decorative border that encircled the classroom. *All* of these people in those dumb white wigs, the ones who had been president, wait, all of them were men? How was this possible? I wasn't a man and I was the smartest kid in the class. I decided that I would be the first female president. It didn't seem out of reach.

ELLEN AND I talked about the day my dad tried to teach me how to ride a bike. Every other kid my age had already learned. It was the summer of 1974 and I was eight and it was time. We were going to take the training wheels off.

Faith had an olive green Schwinn and she'd learned right

away and flew off into the sky every morning on summer weekends when we were free. I had a grape-colored smaller Schwinn with training wheels. It had those red, white, and blue plastic bunches of swishers on the handles, a white basket with a flower on the front, and a loud bell. I rode in squared-off laps, ringing my bell and acting very official and grown up, as if my humongous training wheels didn't give me away.

I finished an imperious final lap and stopped in front of my house, where my dad was standing with a toolbox in his hand.

"You ready?" he asked.

"Yep," I said.

I got off the bike. Handed it to him. He knelt. Opened up the toolbox. He took forever fumbling with the various wrenches. *Which one is it?* Now my hands were on my hips. My sister and her friends were watching. My mom stood with her arms folded, talking to another mom, pretending like she wasn't watching my dad.

Probably another dad came and helped him get the training wheels off—who am I kidding, of course there was another dad, there is no way Harry could have done it on his own.

"There you have it," Bob Powers (not Jewish) probably said as he stood the bike back up.

"Thanks, Bob," Harry said.

Bob Powers went back to his front porch to pretend that he wasn't watching, too.

"You ready?" my dad asked me.

"I'm ready," I said.

My dad ran alongside with his fingers cupping the back

of the seat and everyone was pretending not to watch, including Faith and all of her cool ten-year-old friends. *This should be easy, everyone can do it.*

Off I went, and not even a second passed when I heard him yell, "YOU'RE DOING IT!" That was the *wrong* thing to say—my turned-in knee turned in too much, and the bike began to topple over.

"PUT YOUR FEET DOWN," my dad yelled.

But it was too late. I fell over. Pushed the bike off me.

I can't do this. I can't do this and everyone else can do this.

My dad came over. "You were almost there. You were doing it."

"No, I wasn't." I shoved the bike at him.

"Should we do it again?" he asked.

"I'm done," I said.

"We can do this. Trust me."

"I *would* if you could just *teach* me."

"You won't *let* me teach you. I give up," he said.

My dad picked up the bike and took it back to the house. Set it on our front porch. I dusted myself off and held back tears. Why was something that was so easy for everyone else so hard for me? And how did this become my fault?

Can an eight-year-old be that powerful?

And what does it all mean now? Now that I knew that he wasn't even a man.

THIS HAD BEEN the beginning of a vague pattern of getting to the edge but stopping short. Later that summer, a thwarted swimming lesson at a Michigan resort—the teacher had been paid, but I sat on the side of the pool for half an hour, declaring that nope, I wasn't going in. Years later, I had an audience of pool-goers enthralled as I walked to the end of the high diving board, then turned and climbed down the ladder. Another time, Mom and Dad had to drive to get me from sleepover camp just three days into the planned six-week experience. I felt permanently unbalanced and wiggly legged, unable to push through to the final big good thing. I was always much happier to hold on tight and go backward, one clenched step at a time, down the ladder.

I still don't know how to ride a bike. I have to lie about phantom ankle pain when friends try to get a gang of folks together to bike the river path.

ELLEN AND I finished our session. And then I did what I always do when I'm anxious or confused. I went home and started working.

I am the opposite of most people: for me home is work and work is home. I breathe a sigh of relief when I am buried under the weight of immense work obligations, and I vibrate with anxiety when I imagine this thing called "relaxing" with a "cup of tea."

Despite all this working, many things early in my career just never got made. I'd write stuff, pause, start again, stop, get opinions, ditch, get a new idea, apply to various Sundance labs and programs and contests, get rejected. Almost getting there, thinking I was getting there, and then not getting there. Diablo Cody and Lena Dunham and Jenji Kohan and Tina Fey rising up, up, and away all around me. I tried not to be openly jealous.

The scripts I wrote were always about a complicated female lead—sometimes she owned a florist shop or a burlesque club or was the reluctant PR person to a conservative mayor. She was always a funny/dirty/sad/sex-obsessed/confused dreamer with a name like Sophie or Allie and there were always stars attached. I wrote things for Zooey Deschanel and Marisa Tomei and Lisa Edelstein. Had meetings with Jenna Elfman and Courteney Cox and Rachel Weisz and Christina Applegate and Natalie Portman and Catherine Keener.

One of my first real screenplay gigs was to write a movie about sororities. I worked on the script with the director, Angela Robinson. We wrote the character of Jess, a dorky freshman who didn't fit in and tried to become the person she thought she should be by joining a sorority. Her journey in the movie was to accept her own inner weird girl, grab on to her outsider status. Angela is queer and African American and our hearts filled with a conspiracy to make something wildly commercial with a feminist heart.

After we finished the script, the producer planned a table read so we could hear it read aloud. I sent a few suggestions of actors I thought could read the lead role well, but the producer told me he already had someone fantastic.

After years of work we all piled into a conference room. The actress came in. She looked nothing like the Jess we had been conjuring. She was not an oddball or a misfit or even vaguely dark. She was a super-hot, minuscule blonde. She wouldn't have been able to hit her jokes if her jokes were giant beach balls and her bat was the size of the room. Well, that's not fair; the reason she couldn't hit her jokes was because she was reading them for the very first time when they were coming out of her mouth. She hadn't even reviewed the script before that morning.

I sat there wincing, knowing the project was going down, down, down.

Afterward I pulled our executive aside: *This is a COMEDY. Why can't we have a comedian in the lead? Why did you guys have to pick someone beautiful? This is exactly NOT what this story is about.*

But it was too late, the table read tanked, everyone lost. Two years of my life, gone.

How come Judd Apatow gets to cast Seth Rogen, and all the boys in America get to relate to an imperfect messy human as their protagonist, and I get her?

I didn't fight for anything. I didn't know I could.

But this was normal, right? It was hard to get a movie made.

This scenario continued: projects that seemed like they were going to become something, then never did. Maybe ten or twenty TV pilots, five or more screenplays. What was I doing all those years instead? I guess single-momming my way through life—this was before Bruce—moving up through the world of television writing on other people's shows. Getting there, but saving the juiciest material for my personal dating drama. All the best stuff somehow laminated onto repetitive relationship plots with men: *Did he call? Did you call back too soon? Did he ask you out? Where did he take you? What did you do then? Did you kiss? Did you have sex? Did you have sex too soon? Oh no, did he not call you again?*

Relationships existed to report on them to my friends,

immediately after the door closed after a date. If my love objects were married, all the better. So much wasted energy, all of those stories and plots, poofed into the ether, belonging to any man who came through—that's mostly what I was doing instead of making art. And somehow, over the course of my entire career, I remained comfortable with *almost there*.

Once my parent came out, I was suddenly powered by a huge gust of *yes*. I no longer believed what all of the men said about me, that I wasn't ready. And I stopped believing what I had believed about myself—that I probably wasn't a real artist.

I pulled out an old screenplay I'd started a few years back after a conversation with a friend about what to get our husbands for Father's Day. I was stressing because I had no idea what to get Bruce.

"I know he doesn't want socks or a sweater," I said. "Worst holiday ever."

"You know what my husband would love for Father's Day?" my friend said. "A blow job. A big ol' sloppy twenty-minute blow job from someone who just *loves* giving blow jobs. I wish I could give him that."

We cracked up and I pitched her the absurd notion of looking in the back of *LA Weekly* to find a hooker to help us both out. "Now, *that* would be a Father's Day to remember," we joked.

I started writing a movie based on that premise. I managed to get to page forty—just after the cross from the first act into the second, where all good screenplays go to die— and then I put the script in a drawer.

Something about my parent coming out immediately

shattered a wall; she was being her true self, a woman. Now I could be my true self, a director. I pulled out that old script. *This isn't that bad,* I thought, and renamed it *Afternoon Delight* so as not to callously conflate the beloved American holiday of Father's Day with a sex romp. I holed up and started rewriting, adding pages and pages to the script. I didn't care if they were good pages, I just wanted words and words and more words. I got inside of this mom, this woman Rachel who finds a sex worker out in the world and makes a safe space for her in her house. She lies to her husband and child.

Though I'd started writing it years before my dad came out, as I worked on it now, I realized some part of me must have known subconsciously there had been a woman hiding in our house, too.

I workshopped the script with an amazing theater instructor and theorist named Joan Scheckel. She has introduced many astonishingly simple and effective concepts to actors, producers, directors, and writers over the years. She studied with Stella Adler and reinterpreted Stanislavski's technique of playable actions, imploring us to create characters who ask, "What am I doing to get what I want?" in a scene or story. The answer *always* has to be a verb one can feel.

Within a few days of working together, Joan said, "Jill, your purpose on this planet is to heal the Divided Feminine in our culture." We talked about how women are forced to separate from themselves in order to access male privilege. Men want a good wife, a sweet mommy. In return, a woman gets a house, diamonds, babies, safety. But most women don't want to be limited to one extreme or the other.

Things are more complicated than Madonna versus whore, Betty or Veronica, Ginger and Mary Ann.

Afternoon Delight is about two women, Rachel and McKenna. When two couples go to a strip club, Rachel, a frustrated writer and overthinky stay-at-home mom, gets a lap dance from a stripper named McKenna. In that little hot-pink room where they live inside the hush of intimacy, I swam into Rachel's slow awakening to her awareness of her own Divided Feminine.

Joan helped me see how I could use filmmaking to imagine beyond those projections of good girl and bad girl, mother and slut, virgin and whore. To articulate the uncomfortable need to be seen, and what the whole might contain.

But despite all of these ideas about my own desire to be seen that were informing my work, I still hadn't been to Chicago to visit Carrie. I had the usual excuses: working and momming and how hard traveling was. It had been almost half a year since that phone call.

I finished the script and emailed it to my agent. A fortuitous meeting at the Silver Lake Farmers Market led me to Polly Cohen, who told her friends Jen Chaiken and Sebastian Dungan about the screenplay. They read it and called me the next day.

"We want to make something right away," Jen said. "This is exactly the kind of movie we want to make."

I was in Felix's room, using my turn to sleep late. I bounded out of bed and leapt around on the carpet. I was thrilled, imagining the next year of my life. I was used to telling myself to not get too excited. The conundrum at the heart of life in Hollywood is that you have to believe in your own magic, but not have so much faith that you crash when your project doesn't happen. But I let that adrenaline start to pulse through me. This time, I was going to do it.

A few days later, the three of us sat across from one another in their office in Beverly Hills overlooking Sunset Boulevard. We made an agreement to be done in time for Sundance: "So, we're all saying that if Kate Winslet wants to be in this movie, but says she's not available until January, then we're passing on Kate Winslet." Yup, we shook hands on the idea of passing on Kate Winslet.

Luckily, it didn't matter how Kate Winslet felt, because we never got the script to her. But we did get it to the right actors—in particular, Kathryn Hahn, who would soon become my muse and my friend and my comedy partner-in-crime. We found a line producer and wrote a budget.

I met up with Jim Frohna, a potential cinematographer, at a little French restaurant in Silver Lake. He had long swingy hair and a James Taylor gait and had also worked with Joan Scheckel. We shared the language of playable action. He understood what Joan taught—that the person holding the camera can choose an action, he can *retreat* or *melt* or *murder* with his body, and you would feel it in the frame. I hired him on the spot.

The producers rented me a one-bedroom apartment on a curvy little Silver Lake street for meetings. I made the bedroom into a collage room and covered the walls in the movements of the script. Light sea-foam blue and white stripes of clouds for the first act, hot pink when Rachel meets McKenna, and complex oranges as McKenna weaves herself into the family fabric. Black and sage for when Rachel joins McKenna on an outing to meet a john, deep red for the climax where all the moms get drunk and McKenna has sex with someone's husband, period blood everywhere. The damage is done in Rachel's community and, before long, so is her marriage.

As actors and department heads and collaborators were hired, I invited them over to gather at the apartment. Looking at the walls together, we lived inside a shared version of what the movie would feel like.

I remembered that I'd made a bunch of collages when I was ten and eleven. The tan flesh of male models Scotch-taped onto my walls, making one giant perfect-bodied man. This thing that had seemed like a wasted teenage talent was coming in handy—I was showing myself how I was going to see, as a filmmaker.

The light in the apartment was so soft. Cream walls with the green-gray quality of Fujifilm. Jimmy and I watched John Cassavetes movies on repeat. And I read Cassavetes's manifesto, "What's Wrong with Hollywood," written in 1959, in the mornings, like scripture. In it, he said:

> It is a privilege to communicate worldwide in a world so incapable of understanding. The answers cannot be left in the hands of the money men. The answers must come from the artist herself. She must become aware that art and the respect due this vocation is her responsibility, and that if she cannot garner the respect, the fault is her own.

Of course, Cassavetes didn't say "she"; he said "he," but whatever. Nineteen fifty-nine.

These words propelled me to realize that I had no one to blame if someone didn't see eye-to-eye with me.

Jimmy and I talked about how important it was that

every final decision about casting, writing, shooting, cutting would come from a place of what would make the truest art, and not what people thought would make money. As Cassavetes said, it was our job to make the people with the money want to spend it on our art.

I brought everyone to Joan's and she workshopped in huge groups with the actors and Jimmy. Soon we all had a shared language.

I remember being in downtown L.A., directing on my first day. Kathryn Hahn and Juno Temple leaning against a wall, smoking and talking. Each one had a playable action underneath the dialogue. Maybe Kathryn was playing "admire" and Juno was playing "hide." I'd give Jimmy an action, too. Maybe his was "investigate." When I said "action," we'd roll, and all three would embody their playable actions. Those verbs one can feel became gifts that I handed to the actors between takes. I'd whisper in their ears, *Let's try "melting" instead of "retreating." "Paralyzing" instead of "calcifying."* Every different nuanced playable action resulted in a different performance.

While they were acting, I was feeling. Was it getting close? Closer? What was the new playable action I could suggest to get us there? We taught ourselves something that was part classic narrative filmmaking but also felt like street theater in how it iterated into something new, an opening. Each aliveness illuminating some other element of aliveness. So, okay, filmmaking wasn't about capturing. It was about allowing something to happen.

I learned how to show up without a plan. I'd have a shot list, but no specifics for how things would look or feel. The actors were becoming the characters, and we were documenting this becoming. I was having the time of my life. Finding out that I was capable. Mostly by doing this thing that felt like playing and like breathing. The simple technique of watching the scene and asking, *Does it feel like real life? If not, why not? What can you say to make the moment feel more truthful?*

While we filmed, Jim had a camp counselor vibe, telling the crew, "Let's play games before we start today. Let's all stand in a circle and connect. Make sure we're all on the same page." We realized that standing in a circle was creating the crucible for making art. *Everyone standing here matters. This space between us matters more than a person or a star or the money or a buyer.* This space that would be limerence for two lovers was alive for the whole group of us, and we all just kept folding our soaring hearts back into the batter that was becoming the movie.

3   CLIMBING

SAAC WAS IN HIS SENIOR YEAR OF HIGH SCHOOL AND FELIX WAS IN kindergarten and the bouncy journey of finally claiming the word "director" kept me so busy that I'd barely even noticed that I still hadn't gone to Chicago to meet Carrie.

One day, Faith sent me a text:

—Okay so I finally have a picture of her.
—Of who.
—Of Dad.
—Oh.
—Do you want to see?
—No. Not yet. Oh. Well. Okay fine. Yes. Send it.
—Sent.

I waited for the photo to come up on the phone.

It was a picture of a lovely mature woman who had my dad's face. She was wearing a blond wig, chunky curator jewelry, striped tunic-ish shirt. Carrie. There was a plate of food in front of her. It appeared that she'd had quite a delightful meal. Is that a chicken bone on the side of the plate? I kept enlarging the photo to really get a good look.

Who is this person?

She looked related to us. Maybe like one of my aunts. Big huge smile on her face. I'd never seen my parent smiling quite like that.

I texted Faith:

> —Does she dress this way all the time now?
> What about that wig—will it always be this wig?
> Is she dressing up or is this her?
> —She has a few different wigs. She's just trying on
> different personalities. Like when you're in high
> school. It's normal when you first come out.
> That ebullience. It's called the pink fog.

I wondered what I was supposed to think about the old version of my dad that I remembered. The big one with the beard that wasn't actually dead, but was—where exactly? When I told my friend Nicole about my dad, she said, "Oh, she must be so relieved, to get that big old monkey suit off." But, where was that monkey suit that used to contain my dad? Was it on the floor somewhere, deflated?

The notion got me thinking about my own lifetime of bodily disconnect. I'd gotten my period really late, when I was sixteen, and my breasts seemed to come in an instant a few days later. I had sex for the first time before I'd had my period. I started high school as a girl carrying a purse and putting on lip gloss, and then one summer, I went from genderless child to sixteen-year-old international sex symbol with huge tits. And remember that leg brace I never got? I must have looked like I was flirt-walking down the hallway of Lane Tech High School with my turned-in knee. When my best friend wasn't calling me Crazy Legs, she was calling me Tits on a Stick.

Guys came from everywhere, wise men journeying to behold the glory of my rack. I would be walking down the street on the way to high school, but now cars were stopping, men were leaning out, shouting things. Everywhere, all men did was take me in, let me know I had crossed over to a new country where I was now *in on it* with them. In on what?

Do other peoples' memories of their teenage years include things like soccer competitions or blue ribbons? All I have is the memory of being overwhelmed by watching myself becoming sex to others. My mom had this body, and her mom had this body, and she told me stories of how all the men used to come into the butcher shop they'd owned to look at my Grandma Minnie back when she was in her thirties. She told me this with a guilty twinkle in her eye. I took it to mean *Oooh, you have this, too,* but no directions, no warnings, no discussions about sex. It was more like she couldn't help being proud that I would finally be able to get whatever I wanted, too.

Before long, I got used to the feeling that *all* men were looking at me. I wore my breasts as a weapon and as a shield across my chest, with the awareness that if I performed well for men, I could have anything. I learned how to gain access to power by dangling the possibility of sex, even when I didn't realize I was doing this.

College was me slathering layers and layers of makeup on before I left in the morning. Hair dryers and makeup and red sweaters and drinking—those first few years were all about trying to be in a sorority, hoping not to get caught being different, trying to get close to people who held me at arm's length. I had sex that I never intended to have and disassociated while it was happening. What if everyone just told all college boys that, due to the stress of living on a planet suffering from the gigantic mental illness of misogyny, a lot of girls disassociate when they are learning how to have sex, so please, check in with them a lot to make sure they are still there and consenting?

I guess this is what they call "enthusiastic consent" now. We didn't have that then.

During my junior year at the University of Wisconsin, I took a great women's studies class, developed an intense crush on my k. d. lang–lookalike teacher, and jumped into feminism. It was around the time of the anti-porn demonstrations outside of sex shops. The lights came on. I wrote a paper about how women's pleasure always comes second to men's pleasure. But I got a C for failing to interrogate my own heteronormativity. I cried; it was my first C. I wore less makeup. I noticed how much more time I had in the mornings if I didn't worry about getting my hair right. I dove in harder and deeper, drinking up all the righteous indignation and burning anger on every handout. I turned into a zealot. And I finally met the artists and the hippies—the hairy and the vegan—who would become my people, my real people.

I wanted so badly to be an artist, and to write interesting things, and I decided I would have to have an interesting life if I ever wanted to be like Jack Kerouac. *Submissive to everything,* he got to say, about his technique. I was jealous of him and Neal Cassady and Allen Ginsberg, and it felt so unfair that they could do anything on the road, but if I wanted to go on the road I would get raped. Women spend the first half of our lives afraid we're going to get raped and the second half afraid we're going to find a lump. Are we ever not afraid?

When I had babies, I understood how maybe tears and milk came from the same place, the softness and moistness leaking from connected reservoirs in our bodies. My milk came in with Isaac right away, but with Felix, who was in the NICU and away from me for the first few days of his life, it didn't come until I drank gallons of licorice tea. And even then, it didn't come until the nurses refused to let him go home with me because he hadn't latched on, and I said how is he going to latch on unless I can spend time with him, and I sobbed, and my milk came, and he latched on.

I loved nursing. To feel milk flowing through my breasts made them seem like they were for me, finally. And for my kids. For my family. Because of their size I could do a lot of things while nursing. I didn't even have to concentrate. I could type. But by the time I was done, I was way beyond triple D or F and was probably a size GHX or a ZZY or some other letter that had yet to be invented. I managed to carry my gigantic breasts through the world, somehow always ashamed, not inhabiting my body exactly, but getting on with it. Searching for how to be. Still not riding a bike or being athletic, still opting out of any activity that called for balance or strong legs. I felt like I would topple over under the forward-leaning weight of them. I did whatever mental gymnastics I needed to, to make it so that this thing of being a thing to men also became my thing.

———

WHILE I WAS DIRECTING *Afternoon Delight,* each morning before work, I put on the tightest minimizer. It felt like a cage. I couldn't breathe deeply. I couldn't move quickly. The assistant director would call lunch and I'd drive home. Park the car and run up to my bedroom and strip off my clothes. Run a hot bath. Float. Undo the effects of gravity for twenty minutes. Run back to set and people would say, *Wait, did you just take a shower? Why did you change?*

All of the times I considered changing my body, I came to the conclusion that only a stupid fake real housewife would get cosmetic surgery. I felt pressured to keep my gigantic breasts as a feminist sacrificial act, for women, for all women, for my feminist foremothers, for big women. Andrea Dworkin wouldn't do this, so why am I even thinking about it? How in the world could I take a stand for women and feminism while demanding that all of our bodies are perfectly fine as they are, and cut my own tits off?

At a queer retreat in Mexico, I met Ali Liebegott. She was a poet and a novelist and I instantly worshipped her. She was hilarious like an old Jewish comedian, even though she was neither old nor Jewish. She identified as a lesbian but had gotten top surgery. I was at a beach party with her one day and she hung around with her shirt off. I stared, trying to make sense of things: she wasn't a trans man; she was a dyke with top surgery. I didn't know what that meant, exactly, but I suddenly saw surgery could be a queer thing to do, even before I understood it could be a trans thing to do. There was an evolving sense of reality that said now that I have a *queer* parent, getting my body in line with my mind was no longer just a flight of fancy.

Once the film was finished and submitted to Sundance, I contemplated scheduling breast reduction surgery. I asked around about who was the best plastic surgeon in L.A. The same name kept coming up. His website described him as an artist concerned with aesthetics, a connoisseur of natural appearance. In his photo, he wore a pinstriped three-piece suit and a pocket square that I found simultaneously triggering and reassuring. If he fancied himself an artist, maybe he would make art out of me.

Finishing the film gave me the space to toss and turn around this huge decision. It also cleared my emotional decks, and all the feelings came in, the ones I'd been keeping at bay. I heard that emotional maturity comes from allowing your body to experience feelings before you turn them into thoughts. All I'd been doing was turning my feelings into thoughts and those thoughts into action and that action into work.

Around this time, I had gotten word that Carrie's sister, my aunt Ruth, was nearing the end of her life. My mom had also scheduled hip replacement surgery and needed us. I decided to go to Chicago to say goodbye to Aunt Ruth, be there as my mom went into surgery, and finally meet Carrie.

The plan was that Bruce would stay home with the kids while I traveled. We would arrange a first meeting for Carrie with them one day soon, but for now, only Faith and I were going. By this time, we had told Isaac. He took the news calmly. Most people, including us, still believed that if someone said they were trans, that meant they were getting surgery, and if they weren't getting surgery, well, maybe they were in limbo and maybe none of it would stick. Isaac had nonbinary and genderqueer friends in high school, so it wasn't as dramatic for him as it had been for us. We still hadn't said anything to Felix.

I bought my plane ticket and arranged a car rental. As usual, my parents wanted us deeply embedded in their lives if we went to Chicago. But I was starting to understand how creating a few simple boundaries would provide me with some comfort. I needed to have moments where I could close a door. My mom wants to eat us, to shove us back inside her. Any attempt to be your own person is met by hurt feelings.

I took the red-eye and landed in the morning just in time to see my mom before her hip surgery. She was in great spirits and loved having everyone gathered around her, even if it meant she had to get surgery for this to happen. Once she got out of the operating room, Faith stayed with her while I went to my hotel to check in. It was a few miles away in Northbrook. I parked my big rental Buick in the parking lot of a Something Suites, went to the steak house off the lobby, and sat at the bar. Had a dirty martini on the rocks. Extra dirty. Extra olives. Ordered a steak. Floated as I watched other people eating alone talk to the bartender. Small talk. Should I make small talk? How do people know what to say to bartenders? I stayed invisible in this wood-paneled and amber-windowed place, the view of the gray Kennedy Expressway just outside.

Afterward, I went to see my aunt Ruth. She was in her late eighties. She'd had a full life and although our two families had been close growing up, I hadn't seen her since she'd gotten ill. I'd told her I was coming to Chicago and, through her kids, she asked if she could see me.

I parked beneath some trees at the edge of an expansive golf course adjacent to a forest preserve. Walked through a maze of buildings that looked alike, passed an odd fake pond surrounded by bleating geese. Found my way up to her apartment.

Ruth's hospice attendant opened the door. She was sweet, and the apartment felt warm and quiet. I went to sit at Ruth's bedside. She took sips of water. I told her how much I loved her and how good she looked. Her son David, my cousin, would be there soon. But before he arrived, she wanted something from me. Could I give her my thoughts on a letter she wanted to write my dad?

"What's in the letter?" I asked.

"I don't want him to come to my funeral in women's clothing," she said.

"Okay," I said.

My cousin David arrived. She told him what she wanted to say in the letter and he agreed to write it down as she dictated. Once it was done, maybe I could give it to my dad?

I was so conflicted. She, like my mom, saw my dad's transness as an attention-getting, exhibitionistic ploy. Maybe she didn't want to be upstaged on her big day by what she saw as a dress-up game, even though she wouldn't be there to see it. She also told David and me where to find the extra mustard and Sweet'N Low in the kitchen for the shivah.

I wasn't sure if I could give my dad the card. David said he would.

I went back to my hotel room. There was only one way to get through this, and that was to dive back into work.

I pulled out my laptop and began working on *Transparent*. The script came out so easily, like a slippery baby.

The next night, Faith and I would see Carrie in person for the first time. While my mom was in the hospital recovering from surgery and her husband, Tom, was with her, the three of us were going to have dinner at my mom's house. Faith and I agreed on picking up barbecue to enhance the absurd factor. Moments are always less heavy when people have charred meat in their teeth.

"She's here," Faith said, and went to answer the door. I tried to calm my breathing. I felt hot in the chest, totally fearful as I heard my dad at the door. Her voice had a lilt, but then again, she'd always had a lilt. Maybe we had always been hearing Carrie.

Faith was jovial, her iPhone camera held up, imitating a self-important fashion show narrator, urging Carrie to twirl for us, calling her a supermodel. I felt paralyzed.

We got through dinner somehow. I told Carrie I would drive her home, and we talked a little but it was all too much, my throat closing against the thick smell of an unfamiliar fragrance. Why was she wearing it?

As soon as I dropped her off I started to cry. I called Bruce. He didn't answer. Called Jimmy. He did. I pulled over, cried, and told him everything.

A few days later Ruth passed away. Faith, Carrie, and I took a car to the funeral. David confessed to me that he'd never mailed the card. But Carrie seemed to know anyway. She wore a men's suit, but her nails were pinkish beige and she wore women's loafers and held a small purse. Not a soul noticed.

_____

I LANDED BACK home in Los Angeles just in time to pick up Felix from preschool. As I was climbing the stairs to his second-floor classroom, I saw I had a missed call from a woman named Caroline Libresco, a programmer at Sundance. I hurriedly smushed myself into a corner, put my hand over one ear, and dialed her number. She answered right away and told me the decision was unanimous, that everyone loved my movie and *Afternoon Delight* had been selected into competition. I whooped, then picked up Felix and we went home and I called everyone. Kathryn and Juno and Jimmy. It was real. Everything we had done was for a reason.

That month was a collision of high and low: the pain of Ruth's death and the intensity of Carrie's news and the joy of feeling like I'd made it as a director. I employed my usual coping skill when things got complicated; I made them just a little more complicated.

We had a few months until Sundance. I scheduled my breast reduction surgery.

The night before the operation I took a bath. I asked Bruce to get his good camera so we could take pictures. I cried while I waited, remembering nursing, terrified of the anesthesia, asking Goddess for forgiveness that I was allowing a human man, a mortal in a bespoke three-piece suit, to carve my body into a more efficient shape. I made a plan to go into a recovery center for twenty-four hours following the surgery instead of going home.

Every so often over the years, when I ran into someone I hadn't seen in a while, I'd tell them I'd gotten married, and they would ask about my husband.

"His name's Bruce," I would say. "He's a surfer and a music supervisor and a drummer and amazing and Jewish and brilliant and—"

These people, especially if they were older men, would cut me off, put two hands on my shoulders, look deep into my eyes, and say, "Just tell me one thing, does he take good care of you?"

Um, well. That was the one thing he didn't do. Bruce did a lot of other amazing things. We laughed our heads off. We threw incredible parties. He was great at taking care of Felix. But with me there was a backward rule that I had a chance of getting what I wanted only if I *didn't* ask for it. The two of us lived in a consensual world of non-consent: Jill gets what she wants at work as a director, as an artist. So that's enough for her. Maybe too much.

I could imagine how it would go if I went directly home after the surgery—me not being able to move and needing medicine and having those needs missed or ignored or delayed. Sometimes when Bruce would agree to do something for me, he had to make a show of making me wait an excruciatingly long time to get to it. Could you open the screen door? In a minute, first he had to go downstairs, do the entire year's taxes, then come back up. By then I had opened the screen door myself.

"Why didn't you let me do it?" he would ask.

"I was wanting you to do it when I asked."

The kid who refused to let her father teach her how to ride a bike wasn't going to ask her husband to take care of her either.

The morning of the surgery, my heart was beating fast as Bruce drove us west to Santa Monica. Robin, my old friend from the Gold Coast years, met us there. The doctor did one final exam and used a Sharpie to draw lines on me. I put on a gown and a hairnet and lay down on a gurney. They wheeled me to a room where Bruce and Robin hovered above me. A nurse put a line in my vein and before I had a chance to feel terrified I felt floaty. And then gone.

When I came out of surgery and woke from the anesthesia, only Robin was there. Bruce was at home with the kids. She helped get me into a wheelchair and took me across the street to the recovery center. The room was like a very large ugly hotel room with beige carpet and nurses who checked on you.

I slept through the night, and the next morning Bruce came to take me home. That afternoon my friend Wayne cooked, and Bruce's sister came for dinner, and I lay in bed, listening to a miniature version of a family event go on downstairs without me. I lolled in a state of post-anesthesia depression for a few days.

I finally felt well enough to get out of bed. *Maybe I should see what I've done to myself.* I tiptoed into Felix's room for the light and the full-length mirror. I took off my shirt, my bra, and unwrapped the cloth Ace bandage. I wondered who had put these strange square teenage tits on me. They were so weird, so small, so cute. I felt terrified.

MOUNTAINTOPS

"ONE SECOND!"

I was holed up in a single bathroom in a burger restaurant deep underneath Main Street in Park City, Utah. My friend Jessie pounded on the door.

"WE'RE LEAVING FOR THE SHUTTLE!"

"GO WITHOUT ME!"

"ARE YOU SURE?"

"YES, I'M SURE!"

I needed a little more time because I was busy pulling medical supplies out of my backpack. This was the second time that day I'd changed the gauze inside of my bra. Weeks had passed, but the incision on my left side simply would not close. My mind knew that I needed to heal so I could have fun at Sundance, but my body said *Not so fast, sister.*

Oh, the stories I started telling myself, the shame spiral. Wanting too much, not being satisfied with getting into Sundance. I'd had to go and get surgery, and now look. Why hadn't I bought Hibiclens, the anti-infection soap, when instructed to by my mother? Why had I instead used the brand the surgeon preferred, but only for three days instead of seven, as suggested?

"Nothing to worry about," my dapper doctor had told me over the phone. "You can't even imagine how many people are walking around out there with wounds and dressing under their clothes."

That made me feel a little better. Imagining every single person with bandages and infections under their daywear.

A couple days later it was time for our premiere, which was on a Monday night. By the time we screened the movie I felt like I'd been in Park City for years. Kathryn Hahn and Josh Radnor and Jane Lynch and Juno Temple were all there, and we had our makeup done in the condo. People hired to make the women pretty. I was wearing new clothes, an orange shirt with white polka dots. As I'd hoped, everything fit properly now. I'd also learned to knit in the preceding weeks, anything to stay occupied, and I wore a big pink and orange and red scarf wrapped around my head as we did the media-stop stroll up and down Main Street. We smiled for interviews that may or may not have ever played anywhere. I remember slip-sliding in the slush, running into Jimmy here and my producer Jen there, smashing into a booth with strangers and drinking steamy miso soup. It was like adult summer camp in the snow. It was heaven.

As I leaned on a black speckled countertop in a stranger's Utah kitchen watching the Internet swell with joy over Ryan Coogler's *Fruitvale Station*, I was sure that just after *Afternoon Delight* played on Monday night, we'd have the same kind of juice. A bidding war would commence in Harvey Weinstein's hotel room. I'd be summoned from the after-party to sit across from him while he sold me on why he had to, just had to have it. I pictured him wearing a robe, smoking a cigar. It was a different time.

Everything went as imagined. Well, except for the standing ovation I'd conjured. Instead, we got a partial but in no way conclusive ovation. Was the theater too big? We should have pushed for a different slot, right? Friday instead of Monday? Maybe mistakes were made, but at the party, my agents came rushing up to me, whispering *Awards campaign!* Some buyers from Searchlight were there, or was it Focus? They wanted it, made me promise not to sell it to anyone else, said they'd bring it up at tomorrow's meeting back in L.A. And then asked if I wanted their company SUV to drive my mom and Isaac back to the hotel, and I said of course, and I assumed we were in. Bruce and I danced together.

And then the next day a review came out.

A guy at an important trade paper reamed the film. It was so mean. Even though it was my very first feature, I'd thought I was Cassavetes or at least a young Mazursky, but he'd found it all pedestrian. No big deal here, nothing to see. At its center there's a love story of repression and desire between two women but he'd missed it, or simply didn't care. It cast a chill over everything.

Look, I'm not saying that the movie was a masterpiece. Okay, truth be told, I thought it was a masterpiece, but all artists think that about their own work. That's how we get through, we're alternately genius and despicable, and I had absolutely thought I was making something brand-new. We have to have delusions of grandeur to get anything done, right?

And, of course, I wondered what the review would have been like if a woman had been assigned to write it.

One reviewer can write "a great new voice in American

filmmaking" and a career is born. A reviewer can say "meh" and a career stalls out. Men reserve these whooshing genuflections for their bros, their nerd buddies.

Lili Loofbourow writes about this male glance, this disdain for our work:

> The male glance is the opposite of the male gaze. Rather than linger lovingly on the parts it most wanted to penetrate, it looks, assumes, and moves on. It is, above all else, quick. Under its influence we rejoice in our distant diagnostic speed. . . . It feeds an inchoate, almost erotic hunger to know without attending, to omnisciently not-attend, to reject without taking the trouble of the analytical labor because our intuition is so searingly accurate it doesn't require it. . . . Closer to the amateur astronomer than to the explorer.

A female critic I knew characterized the reviewer who reamed me as a man who reviews the date-ability of the lead actress. He felt my film deserved nothing more than the most glancing glance from him, a farted *pfft* review out of the side of his mouth.

I've since had tearful calls from filmmakers over the years after reading his disdainful reviews. Trade papers publishing this stuff. Ruining careers. On one movie, Spike Lee asked that only black critics review his work. I wish I could do something similar. For all women. I was furious.

I was still at Sundance and stuck in my bedroom. I couldn't move. I went to rock bottom in a fog of dread-and-shame flu. Hot heat on. Cold, cold snow piled outside. A paralyzing daymare that I'd died. I was asleep in a drawer at the morgue. There were so many drawers, it looked like the big brass mailbox wall in the lobby of our apartment building back in Chicago. There were bodies in all the mailboxes.

I finally got out of bed and went to dinner. Tried to put on a brave face. Hahn was looking for me. She was ruined, too. Shattered.

Everyone else had already gone back to L.A., including my cousins from Virginia and Faith. Isaac was back at high school. Felix and Bruce and his parents had left.

The town had mostly cleared out.

I was ready to ditch Park City, blaming the forecasted storms instead of admitting to the size of my crash. I'm afraid I might get stuck here, I told people casually. Did you see the news? Lotsa snow coming, we may get socked in. I think I'm going home early.

My friend Michaela convinced me to stay for the awards ceremony. We Ubered through the snowy night to a gymnasium a few miles away that had been transformed into a violet-lit party space. We sat at long, rectangular tables, straining to stay attentive in the clangy room. When Ed Burns called out my name for the best director award, I couldn't believe it. I walked up, incredulous, and shook my head as he handed me the award.

As we walked off stage, I said to him, "I got the worst review of my life yesterday."

He said, "Welcome to being a grown-up artist. Now you begin."

AFTER GETTING HOME from Sundance, I was ready to pitch *Transparent*. The pilot script was finished. My agent and I made a plan. I would go in and see each buyer and tell them the real-life story about my parent, and then he would send over the script.

I'd put in many years as a writer on shows at HBO and Showtime, so I was sure that both places would want their favorite daughter to stay in-house. Heck, maybe Netflix would get in on the action, and I could land a deal that involved some kind of a series commitment. A bidding war would ensue! This was only a few months after the non-bidding war that never ensued at Sundance so I have no idea why I was so good at convincing myself that one was coming.

I still had the photograph of Carrie in the blond wig that my sister had sent me. I got dressed in my writerly finery, with some loose curls delicately placed with a narrow curling iron to appear tousled just so, minimal makeup, and something that looked like a business suit. Over the course of a few days, I went to all of the usual suspects—HBO and Showtime and FX—and pitched my heart out. The conversations went something like this:

What have you been up to? Uh-huh. Uh-huh. Sundance? Wow. The directing award? Awesome.

So, I have some news, I would say. *I got a phone call from my dad not long ago.*

I told them about the coming-out moment, the phone call that starts this book. Then whipped out the iPad and showed the photo.

There was lots of amazement. Shock.

She looks so happy, so many of them said.

Back then, I didn't know about the politics of outing people. I was showing my parent's picture without her consent. But it felt worth it. I had this one-dimensional doll of her hiding inside my iPad to spring on everyone at just the right moment.

It's okay, right, Carrie? To show you to all of these people you don't know? Before you answer, know that I'm doing it to be able to make everything you told me all okay with art, and these people might even pay for it! You say yes, right?

Was it unfair to transform my real life into a product? Is it possible that snatching and grabbing the image of my parent was a way of getting back at Carrie for pulling Faith in so tight while I was way over there? When I was growing up, they were the Real Artists, gathering around the piano, the only two in the house who could hear pitch. They teased me and my mom for being off-key so much that neither of us attempted to sing. Sometimes I would join them and they would start laughing.

The sooner-to-be-queer Soloways, Faith and Carrie, were the embodiment of music and art, and I don't know why, but I wasn't. They were different and my mom and I were normal. I was expected to thrive academically, but Faith, my mom always said, marches to her own drummer. She never added "and Jilly marches to my drum," but I think that's what she meant. We lived in a divide: Mom and Jill are cute PR capitalist machines, and Faith and Dad are the real thing, tortured and musical and filled with longing and melancholy melody.

I WENT TO FIVE or six places to pitch the show, but each place passed. HBO seemed interested, but they were in the midst of a regime change. Sue Naegle, who'd discovered *Girls*, was on her way out. The inside word was that even if HBO said they liked my show and wanted to buy it, the chances that it would ever see the light of day were slim. I was excited to go to Showtime, but they passed. There had been some drama left over from *United States of Tara*. The job had been a political shitshow; each year, a different showrunner fought for power. One year I somehow won and took over, but by the next year two dudes had knocked me out again. I was persona non grata, or, as Faith and I say—au gratin—at Showtime. The folks at FX apologized—they had been developing a show called *Pretty/Handsome* about a family with a trans dad with Ryan Murphy and even though the project was stalled, they really didn't want to offend him. Netflix felt that *Orange Is the New Black* was their trans show, so they opted out. Each phone call from Larry, my agent, was *It's not gonna happen there. I'm so sorry. It didn't go our way.*

Finally, Larry called to let me know there was one more option. Amazon wanted to hear the pitch. The place I did my online shopping for banana slicers and replacement phone chargers wants to make my show into a web series? No. Thank. You.

I went to the meeting anyway. Amazon shared a weird, giant open office with IMDb. It was in an industrial-airplane-hangar-type start-up spot above the Sherman Oaks Galleria. I sat down with Joe Lewis, Sarah Babineau, and Kristen Zolner. They all seemed to be about twenty-four years old. Did these childlike people really have something to offer me?

They explained to me that no, it wouldn't be a web series, that their budgets would be the same as any TV network.

Okay, really? And what channel would it be on?

It would be on Amazon.

Hmm.

I thought about what I had just been through with the movie business, where you start with nothing, not one dollar, then you use the script and the actor commitments to raise money, then hustle more money out of investors by showing them early cuts and letting them give you advice and promising them good times at Sundance.

Then, once you play at a film festival, you spend all your time hoping you don't get any poor reviews, but if you get just one, you struggle to find a distributor who will pay back even part of what you spent. If that comes up short, you send the film to international markets to make up your losses. At that very moment, in those very markets, *Afternoon Delight* was being passed like a corpse from man to man, male buyers and sellers, all apologizing. *I'm sorry, we couldn't sell it. I'm sorry, it hasn't made enough money.*

If nothing else, by trying this version of whatever they were calling TV with Amazon I'd at least have the funding to get started on something.

They were my last option. I went from being highly suspicious to selling them hard: "If you liked *Afternoon Delight*," I said to Joe Lewis, "I can make a pilot that feels very similar. I have the cinematographer and editor and the hair and makeup person and the costume designer to make it look the way that movie looked. I have a technique, around playable actions, that I use with actors. I know how to get the kinds of performances you saw in the film. Most people who come in to see you with a script can't guarantee much by the time a director and a producer get involved; the tone can evaporate right before your eyes. As writer, director, and producer, I can guarantee the tone."

Somehow, even though my movie felt like nowhere near enough of a success, it was something I could point to. It was a way for people to know my voice. I left the meeting calm; this just might work. Who knows what would come of it, but at least I'd be back in production soon, behind the camera.

I called my agent after the meeting.

"Okay, so I'm not sure about these people," I said. "Or their weird offices. And what if I shoot the pilot with Amazon, and nothing comes of it? I don't think I'm ever going to have a story like this again."

Larry proposed an idea. "What if," he asked, "I get them to agree that if they pass on the TV show, you can have the footage back so it can be the first half hour of your next feature?"

"Genius," I said.

Larry went back and forth and back and forth, fighting for this. Finally, Amazon agreed—as long as they had right of first refusal on the movie.

A few days later it appeared that the deal was getting under way. I started thinking about casting. I knew I wanted Gaby Hoffmann to play Ali. I had met her at a women's dinner at Sundance, and after seeing her on *Louie*, talking a mile a minute, I'd become obsessed. She was in a movie at Sundance called *Crystal Fairy*. She was so comfortable with her body. Wild and running free with her thick eyebrows and wide stance on the big screen.

We had gone out for sushi in Park City and I asked her if she would play the role. She didn't know if anything would come of it. But she said yes. Now, a few months later, I was calling her for real.

Can you do it? Amazon wants to make it.

Amazon the shopping place?

Yep.

After Amazon made the offer, they wanted to know who I was thinking of for Maura.

I just wasn't sure which man would be right.

It never even occurred to me to cast a trans woman.

Lists were made. Kevin Kline and John Larroquette and all of the men I had grown up watching on TV and in movies.

Isaac and I were driving somewhere and listening to Marc Maron's *WTF* podcast. Jeffrey Tambor was on, live from SXSW, teaching a class about acting. We laughed our heads off. Jeffrey's sense of humor was exactly the same as my dad's. Over the years, when I had seen him on TV, he had always felt so familiar to me. Way back when I'd written my first-ever spec script for TV, it was a *Larry Sanders* episode with a main story line about Hank getting wrapped up in a multilevel marketing scheme selling lotion. I understood his cadence and his nuance; he looped deep into my epigenetic comedy past. Jeffrey had to be Maura.

I called my agents and they called his agent and a breakfast was arranged at Le Pain Quotidien in the Valley within a day. I watched him get out of his big SUV. He was taller than I had thought. Around the size of my dad.

He came into the café and we hugged. *I'm in, I'm in, I'm*

in, he said. I needed a second. I didn't know how it worked. I didn't know if Amazon would just let me have anyone I wanted, but it didn't even take a day; they were thrilled. Jeffrey was cast.

I called Carrie and told her. She loved Jeffrey Tambor. *Perfect!* she said.

None of the women on the short list to play Shelly lived in L.A. They were all New York theater actors—Patti LuPone, Andrea Martin, and Tovah Feldshuh. I scheduled Skype calls with everyone. When I saw Judith Light's name on the list, I wasn't sure. She didn't seem Jewish at all. I checked in with Faith, who had been playing adjunct casting director, along with Isaac. Faith went nuts when she heard Judith was interested.

"It's her, it's her, it's her," Faith implored over the phone.

I did some research and found out she actually was Jewish and from New Jersey. It was her long blond hair that had been throwing me off; I asked if she would she cut her hair. NO! she said, but of course she could wear a wig. I didn't know then how good they could make wigs.

Judith and I Skyped. She was so delightful and loving and lovey, pouring out her heart, telling me why she had to play Shelly. She was on the board of the Point Foundation, a nonprofit that mentored queer and trans college students. She was beloved in queer communities for decades for her AIDS activism. I got Amazon to send out the offer as soon as we hung up.

Next, it was time to cast Sarah. I called Kathryn Hahn to check in. I had offered her the role when we were making *Afternoon Delight.* She had given me a resounding yes, but now things had changed. She had just signed on at Showtime to do a TV show with Philip Seymour Hoffman and was no longer available.

It took a few days for me to get over what felt like a betrayal. I started to think about another actress from *Louie*— Amy Landecker. She was from Chicago and felt so familiar and hilarious and most of all so real. So human. I tried to schedule a meeting but she passed because the part called for possible nudity. I tried to sway her by sending her *Afternoon Delight,* hoping she might like my crack at reimagining how it felt to be those 1970s boy auteurs, inventing ourselves through film. She agreed to meet. We went to Viet Noodle Bar in Atwater Village and sipped hot pho.

She loved the movie, she said. She was in.

My heart soared as this group came together. But we had only a week or so before we were supposed to start shooting the pilot and the role of Josh was still uncast. I could see him in my head—his beardy, oh-so-adorable Jewy ways.

One night I was invited to a directors' dinner, where people share off-the-record thoughts about working, techniques, gossip, life on set. Ruben Fleischer would hold them every few months at his house in Los Feliz, and it would usually be me plus forty-nine men.

Where were all the women directors hiding? Why hadn't they been inviting us? Were we all at home nursing our babies and watching the Kardashians?

I was outside on the back deck, munching pizza and trying not to make any gang-rape jokes, when a guy walked in. *That,* I thought, *is exactly what Josh should look like.* I asked someone else who he was and they said, "One of the Duplass brothers. Jay, I think."

A few moments later Jay was next to me munching pizza.

In the middle of a conversation about casting *Transparent,* I said, "It's you. He's you." He was mostly a director and was too busy creating his own show, *Togetherness,* for HBO.

He suggested a few other actors. "How about David Krumholtz? People are loving him again."

"No, not him," I said.

He tried a few more suggestions.

"At least come in and audition," I said.

The next morning, he did. We tried the dinner scene from the pilot with Gaby and Amy. It was like the room levitated when they were together. But Amazon didn't want him in second position to his HBO show; HBO could pull him out of our shooting schedule at will. I got on speakerphone with the folks in business affairs and paced around the room, waving my hands, monologizing, hoping to share my vision. This would be something I would learn I'd have to do over and over again as a leader. Get on the phone. Speak the truth from deep in my gut. Say to people, *Trust me, it's going to be okay.*

I. Just. Knew. Just like they say about soul mates. Just like I had felt about Bruce. But this was a new family. We all ran straight into one another's arms and nobody was running away. These people were real. The Pfeffermans were alive.

5   TAKING HER OUT FOR A SPIN

IABLO CODY TOLD ME THAT THERE WAS THIS THING THAT HAP-
pened when she made *Juno*. She could feel it as she was
writing the script, the words pouring out, and then when
the writing was done, she didn't have to hustle. The project got swept up on an upward ride, a succession of yeses
that took her straight through production to publicity to the
moment onstage where she waved her Academy Award in
the air.

I had been working steadily for over a decade. Year after
year, I would write two or three pilots, and they would always sell but never actually get made. So many projects were
always SO CLOSE, and yet . . . Nothing. Ever. Happened.

Now it was happening. I finally had a successful script
about an unlikable Jewish chick—but it turned out I needed
a man to play her to get it there.

As we were getting ready to start filming, I thought
about Rhys Ernst, a trans filmmaker I'd met at Sundance.
He was really sweet and the whole time I was with him I
wanted so much to tell him about my parent. But I was too
embarrassed. I kept trying to figure out what the opening
sentence would be. If I went up to him and started talking

about transness immediately I would seem like I was to-kenizing him. I knew he was trans, but I didn't know if he knew that I knew.

But now that the pilot was happening, I had a real job offer to make. I asked my friend, the artist Elana Mann, to introduce me to Rhys as well as Zackary Drucker, an artist, photographer, and experimental filmmaker from Los Angeles. They had just found out a photo series they'd worked on was going to be in the Whitney Biennial. They came over and we sat around the big wooden farm table. Their trans-ness was still a novelty to me. Having them visit felt important, like they were emissaries from a delegation of very special people. I was afraid of coming off like a boring sub-urban mom. We talked about the potential of the show. I in-vited them to be collaborators on the journey. They said yes.

"There's one more thing we have to do," Zackary said. "Find Maura."

She asked me whether Jeffrey had "taken her out for a spin" yet.

No, not yet.

WE PICKED A NIGHT in the fall of 2013. Earlier that evening, I did a Q&A at a theater in Westwood for *Afternoon Delight*. The movie had ultimately found a distributor and a few weeks of theatrical release. But we had to work our asses off to get people to see it. We were absolutely in the wrong place at the wrong time with that movie—it was a year or so before there was any real business model for selling mov-ies to Netflix and no one had any ideas about how to get people to care about cinema that wasn't a tentpole super-hero movie.

The screenings were always great. I've always wished I could only gauge my work through the eyes of feminists and artists and Soloway fans and Jewish people instead of dismissive male reviewers. I loved doing the Q&As and looping together my Divided Feminine themes about vulnerability and truth-telling. But as soon as this Q&A ended, I had somewhere I needed to be.

I jumped in my car and drove west to the hotel where Jeffrey was staying. Jimmy was going to meet me there to document the transformation with his still camera. I got to the hotel and went to the room number they gave me. Rhys and Zackary were there, in the bathroom with Jeffrey.

I mean Maura.

There she was, in the wig we had gotten from the hair and makeup department. I exhaled. She was so real.

"My mom used to say my mouth doesn't make sense," Jeffrey said, staring in the mirror at Maura's mouth. "It finally makes sense."

Her mouth did make sense, a little angel bow of a smile turned up in the corners, not right on a man but very familiar in lipstick. Zackary was smoothing the sides of her hair as we all took Maura in. Her long grayish brown hair parted on the side. Eye shadow. Defined eyebrows. Zackary had asked Marie Schley, our costume designer, for some outfits. Jimmy clicked photos as we all hovered. Jeffrey was shy. He stood up. Pushed back from the dressing table. Walked around the room. She was beautiful.

It was time to go dancing.

We gathered our things and walked through the lobby. Jeffrey was petrified. But no one, not one person, stared or cared. We got in our cars and drove to the deepest valley; it was Club Shine at the Oxwood, a night for T-girls, as they used to be called, and it had been going on weekly for eleven years. As I pulled up, the security guard excitedly shooed me away from a parking space he was saving for Judith Light. Yes, Judith Light was on her way! Do you remember her from *Who's the Boss?* and *One Life to Live*, he asked.

I parked in a different space and went in. Jeffrey, Rhys, and Zackary had already arrived. It was dark and purple and neon inside like any seedy nightclub. The place was almost full with a diverse group of trans women, plus some older cross-dressers. One who was British and introduced herself to me and told me that no one at work knew this side of her.

Did Carrie go out clubbing to places like this? I wondered.

No one recognized Jeffrey. When Judith arrived, a few people recognized her. We all sat against the wall in a leather banquette, trying to be inconspicuous. Lady Gaga was singing "Bad Romance." We all got up to dance. Jeffrey started out slow. Then let go. We went nuts together. I filmed it on my iPhone; Jimmy took pictures. Maura was free.

MARIE HAD BEEN our costume designer on *Afternoon Delight*. This would be her first department head gig on a television show. She made astonishing mood boards for each character. They were like paper dolls with outfits to pick from. I loved going through all of the options and approving wardrobe. Cat Smith was the production designer. She had been second in command on *True Blood*, and *Transparent* was her first time leading the charge. She found the Pfefferman house. It was a real house in Pasadena, but we shot it to play as if it was on the west side of L.A. in the Pacific Palisades.

When Jeffrey was dressed as Maura he felt like an accessible version of my dad. One I could go to a nightclub with. Be tender. Maura would smooth the hair out of my eyes. Notice my bad mood. *Are you okay?* she would ask. As an adult, I never would have been this intimate with Carrie. She was still too foreign. Our family's never been good with physical contact anyway. I used to watch Bruce's parents tickle their grandkids' backs and couldn't understand what anyone was thinking.

On the Sunday before we started shooting, I had the cast over to my house for brunch. I opened the French doors, and Felix and Isaac and Bruce mixed in with the people who played Maura and Shelly and Josh and Sarah and Ali— Jeffrey and Judith and Jay and Amy and Gaby. The birds were chirping and people were moving in and out of the house like real family. Jeffrey sat on the couch and put his feet up and read the paper, then fell asleep.

A few days later, we had our first table read. Everyone gathered in a big room at Paramount. We took a collective deep breath. I talked about the notion of creating a show that would make the world safer for my parent. I offered up an idea I had thought of the night before in the bathtub and told myself *say it don't say it say it don't say it*, but in the room with everyone, something inside me just said *fuck it say it*, so I said: "On most shows, they act like they're running out of money, they're running out of time, they're running out of light. On this show, let's try saying we have plenty of money, we have plenty of time, and we are the light."

It was corny and enthusiastic and earnest, but it worked. We read the pilot aloud. The room felt like it was alive and vibrating. Faith was there; she had an electric piano and at the end she played the Jim Croce song "Operator." Everyone sang along. Some of us cried. We were launched.

Over the next five days, we shot the pilot at a bunch of locations—the Pfefferman house in Pasadena, in Griffith Park, Len and Sarah's in Studio City, Ali's little apartment in an ornate old building called Los Altos in Koreatown. I'd spent time in my twenties at a similar Hollywood building called the Villa Carlotta. Both were 1940s buildings with romantic lobbies and gigantic palms in the courtyards, adorned with colored Christmas lights. The kind of building you find only in L.A., filled with sour people who'd almost made it as movie stars, failed homecoming queens, scruffy, alcoholic would-be novelists.

We also shot Shelly's condo in an apartment complex in Marina del Rey. As I looked around at the place we'd chosen, I recognized it from somewhere. Oh that's right, it was just like the place in Buffalo Grove where I'd visited my aunt Ruth just before she died. I began to realize that my perceptions about needing to bring something great to my work were wrong. There was nothing I needed to get or know or bring with me. Artists synthesize their experiences onto the canvas, the page, or the screen. Everywhere we'd all been, all the people we'd met and the inside jokes we have, we sculpt them into what we make. Filmmaking was revealing itself to be a permission structure for me to re-create places and moments from my life. Relive them. It is so many things, but sometimes it is simply a nostalgia factory.

As a director, I wove in techniques I'd learned at the Annoyance Theatre in Chicago, back when Faith and I were putting on live episodes of *The Brady Bunch* just after college in the early nineties. More versions of pretend families.

When we were little, Faith and I lived and breathed *The Brady Bunch*. Every night as we fell asleep we would play a game where one of us would say a line from an episode, and the other one had to name the episode. I had a strange but intense yearning to meet Eve Plumb and ask her what it was like to be Jan. How do people treat you? Is it weird for people to think you're Jan? Did growing up as Jan turn you into Jan? Did you ever really put lemon juice on your freckles? I wanted to interview all of the Bradys about how it felt to be those characters to so many people right when you were figuring out who you were.

The Real Live Brady Bunch, our theatrical version, had a secret chewy center that comedically shamed the rest of us for not being loving or gender balanced or brown-blond balanced. Amping up the laugh track to remind the live audience of how we all laughed along at their manufactured perfect imperfections when we watched as kids. Our Annoyance Theatre company became another family, putting on more and more shows like it was a clubhouse. A dream cult.

We'd had our own dad at that theater, another guru, Mick Napier. He had a few rules about creating. The first was a major tenet of improv: *Yes, and.* Go with whatever is happening, allow the soul of the *us* to expand, rather than insist on some very particular path. He reminded us to privilege process over product. If the *way* we do things has integrity, we will be making art. He encouraged us to give gentle feedback using the word "could" instead of "should." On show nights, he would remind us never to discuss *if* something was good, but rather to celebrate *that* it had happened. It was bad juju to talk about a producer or a critic who came, no matter their reaction. We were absolutely not to rank the experience before it had a full chance to breathe and become itself. I brought as much as I could of this to our process on *Transparent*.

We'd used some of this mentality on the set of *Afternoon Delight,* where Jimmy and I had created space for just being there to witness whatever happened. Our crew was used to this, but our *Transparent* actors were accustomed to being told where to stand and how to say their lines. Everyone felt like they were back in theater school. Playing. Being in the flow.

The climax of the pilot is a scene around the table, everyone eating barbecue takeout. Maura has gathered all of her children. Her plan is to come out to them. Like everything else, the scene wrote itself, but now that I was here, watching the prop people re-sauce rib after rib, I remembered that when I'd met Carrie for the first time at my mom's house, there was sauce everywhere. Faith and I had wondered whether Carrie would eat barbecue differently than Harry had. We re-created this moment when Sarah and Ali had to decide whether they would tell Mort that he had food on his face, an inside nod to the absurd expectation that women are naturally more dainty when they eat. Can you be a lady and have food on your face? I didn't think about this then, but I think about it now as I attempt to find more meaning in this intersection of gender and desire, appetite and messiness, and how Carrie crossed over, even though we didn't want to let her. We wanted the ability to eat prettily to be a test.

We used a round table with a camera in the middle that slowly spun, mimicking a Martin Scorsese shot that captured everyone. It was meant to arouse a feeling of nausea in the audience, the too-muchness of the worlds colliding. In the original script, Maura had come out at dinner, but Joe from Amazon wanted me to change it so that Maura pulled back at the last minute. I compromised by still having Maura come out at the end of the pilot—to the viewing audience, but not to the children.

Instead of announcing that she was transitioning, Maura would announce that she was selling the house. The formal notion behind the series was now clear—the kids would believe they were inheriting their family home, but instead they would inherit a legacy of queerness.

After we finished the last day of shooting the pilot, we hugged, deeply dreaming that we would all soon be back.

I edited the episode and waited for Amazon to release it. In those days, they were letting America watch and decide which series should and shouldn't be picked up.

Bruce was working with me as a music supervisor. When I was writing the pilot I had called out, "What's a band like ABBA, that everyone's ready to rediscover, but less pop and more meaningful?" And he called out, "Jim Croce," as he carried a laundry basket from one room to the next. He made me playlists to write to and one of the songs, "Mayla," by Edward Sharpe, ended up getting played over and over again on set and then became a major piece of music in the pilot, just at the moment when Maura emerged from Mort and let down her hair and put on her nightgown and got into bed to read. The hushed soft voice singing, *Mayla long time / May the sunshine / Hold on we're trying / Our hands are bleeding through / We're building us a new horizon.*

In the weeks after the pilot was done, I reconnected at home. Bruce always knew the right songs to play in our house. From the first night we'd had Shabbat dinner together and he'd made a playlist of songs from my collection that I didn't even know I had, I heard those Jeff Tweedy lyrics and believed they meant Bruce knew me. But now he was making playlists for the show instead of burning devotional CDs to our love. I didn't think this mattered—there were no boundaries between my family and the TV show family, and the playlists and the music on the set and the music in the cut. I was learning how to ride this thing that felt as big as the earth, to allow the connections to be made and just try to stay on top.

The Pfeffermans existed as a better version of our family. Some of the best actors I had ever met read the words on the page and adopted the character names and somehow found live souls. The Pfeffermans were a monument to a fantasy about respectability. A fantasy I didn't realize I needed until I got this surrogate projection, this one that was so pleasing to behold. It began to overtake real life.

As soon as I finished editing the pilot, I flew to Chicago to show it to my parents. Faith came in from Boston, and I got us a hotel room to share. Our parents' boundarylessness was more intense now that Carrie was constantly transforming. Every time we saw her in those first few years there would be a new look, a new voice, a new Carrie. She wasn't a show I could write and direct. She was unbearably real.

Our hotel room didn't have a DVD player so my mom had us all over to her apartment. We gathered in her tiny one-bedroom, high in the sky, overlooking downtown Chicago. Both of my parents live like college students, just enough room for themselves. Was it our Soloway lot to be satellites jettisoned to different corners of the world, Faith and I on either coast, Elaine and Carrie in the middle, every one of us alone in our safe spots, titrating our anxiety? Did other families have gatherings in big houses with wrap-around porches in Michigan? Barbecue dinners at round tables in mid-century modern Pacific Palisades post-and-beam havens?

I tried to shove the DVD into the player but it wasn't working. Was this screening even going to happen? My parents didn't know what this was yet. Neither did I, really. Was it a web series? Amazon was going to "play" it? Would anyone actually see it?

Truth be told, Carrie probably would have preferred that no one ever saw it. I remembered that she had called me only a few months before, wondering if I could make the family not Jewish, maybe make the dad a fireman, anything to disguise the Soloways. She was anxious and unsure about having our family name connected in any way to transness.

"People hate trans people, you know," she told me. "We can't even walk down the street."

But that is why I made it, I thought. To hurry up and change the world. Like when Superman flies around and around the earth with his rope, slowing down the turning of the planet. Except in my mind, I was trying to make the world move forward so that what was happening in the present would feel tolerable for my parent. And me.

The DVD player wouldn't work, but I found a way to pull up the cut on my laptop. My mom streamed it to her monitor. We gathered close, sitting on the floor.

My parents talked over the actors' dialogue in the beginning, but they had always done that when watching an episode of something I'd written. I always thought it was made of solid gold and had to be listened to intently; I used to shush them when we watched my *Six Feet Under* episodes together.

At the moment in the pilot when Maura relaxed to that Edward Sharpe song, something shifted in the room. On-screen there was a move to another slowly turning camera—the frame landing on Maura, proud, at her support group, surrounded by other trans people, talking about her family. She's finally herself, for the first time in the pilot, and she looks good, and when Carrie saw her, she quietly said, "Oh, there she is."

Maura looked through the camera and asked what she had done to make such selfish children.

The pilot ended and I turned it off.

I turned to face my family. Faith had tears in her eyes. So did I.

My mom seemed to like it but didn't have anything to say just yet.

But Carrie had a question.

"Jilly?"

"Yes," I said, expecting something huge.

"What did they pay for the house?"

Faith and I exchanged looks. There was a line in the

middle of the pilot when Shelly complained about her divorce settlement and mentioned that they had bought the Palisades house in 1984 for $52,000.

That's the part Carrie was curious about.

There was no sobbing, no *You really see me*, no *Wow, you're an amazing artist, Jilly, you've finally done it and you're going to change the world.*

I said, "It's not real, Dad, it's a script."

Faith and I were so sure our parents would be transformed by the art, but Carrie was who she was, wondering: *Wait, who are these phantom people who have a similar life to us? Because I don't think that's what we paid for our house.*

MAZON WAS JUST GETTING STARTED AS A NETWORK SO THEY were galloping to catch up to how the TV business worked. But they loved the show and had so much passion for it, and that felt so alive it was more than enough. The buzz surrounding the casting, writing, and shooting was so positive that they gave us the go-ahead to start hiring writers and working on the season, so that we would be ahead of the game if they wanted to pick it up straightaway.

Every TV writer who has sat in a writers' room under the leadership of a showrunner has created an imaginary dream staff in their mind. I had been waiting my whole career for a good reason to hire Faith. She had proven herself as an awesome songwriter and comedian, but she had never quite got it together to write a spec script, which is the equivalent of a headshot in the world of screenwriting. In this case, even if she didn't have the writing sample, she did have the knowledge of every absurd and deep feeling of what it meant to be a Soloway, an ur-Pfefferman. I called her to drop a bomb—can you move to L.A. in a few weeks to start working? She wasn't sure if she could, because she had made a commitment to be a summer camp counselor.

A few hours later she said, *What the fuck am I even thinking, YES! I'm coming!*

I knew I wanted to hire Ali Liebegott, the genderqueer poet who reminded me so much of all the old Jewish comedy guys I'd ever worked with. I happened to randomly catch a Facebook post that she was contemplating moving from San Francisco to Long Beach, so I instant-messaged her about the gig. My assistant on *Afternoon Delight*, Ethan Kuperberg, was an amazing writer and I knew he was ready. I was friends with another brilliant Ivy League–ish Jewish fellow named Micah Fitzerman-Blue and had been trying to work with him and his writing partner, Noah Harpster, for a while. They got the call next.

None of them had worked in television before. Amazon was worried—shouldn't I get at least one person who had done this before? I met with Bridget Bedard, who had just come off *Mad Men*. We had a great get-to-know-you interview in my kitchen. The last question I asked her was why she wrote. She thought about it and then said, "Well, I can't really think of much of a reason to wake up if I'm not writing." She got the job.

We moved into our writers' offices, which we called the Honeycomb Hideout. It was a strange, two-story art studio on Silver Lake Boulevard that conveniently had bedrooms upstairs. Faith, Ali, and our new production assistant John Biggers didn't have a place to live, so they moved in. We wrote downstairs; they lived upstairs. It was a commune, the kind of Utopian dream camp Faith and I had been re-creating ever since South Commons.

Living amid a large group, like the real or imagined Brady Bunch or an imaginary dynasty of WASPs at their summer lake house, or maybe just a troupe or a circus, is home to me. I've always felt safest in these kinds of groups. There seems to be a sifting system that commands everyone's best behavior, and also justly calls out misbehavior. It was in smaller groups, like couples or families, where the pressures of inventing a moral framework moment to moment intimidated me.

There was only one problem—as somewhat queer as that group sounds, we still didn't have a trans woman writing on the show, a show with the word "trans" in the title. From my perspective now, it's clear I was unconsciously protecting my privilege. I see cis men doing this all the time when asked to diversify the people with whom they make the most important decisions about their work. But at the time, I just wanted the room to feel like home.

Rhys contacted Jenny Finney Boylan, who had published a memoir called *She's Not There: A Life in Two Genders* and was one of the first people to humanize the complexities of transness through her beautiful prose. We needed to hire someone who could give us the late-transitioner perspective, and she was close to Maura's age. We asked if she was interested in coming aboard as a consultant. Her initial response was a fast *no*. We seemed to be just another random web series about trans people from a cis person's point of view, probably comedy-izing and commodifying transness for profit. She said she probably wouldn't be able to work on it with us, but she would watch the pilot.

Soon after, she sent me an email:

> Holy Fucking Cow. It's brilliant. It strikes me as a
> lyrically and brilliantly constructed work of art.

> The trans issues are hardly even the point. The
> characters, especially the siblings, are complexly
> and subtly created. The editing is gentle and
> lyrical. The whole thing is darkly, softly funny, and
> full of love. I would be thrilled to work with you.

We arranged for her to come to the writers' room to help ground the character of Maura for us.

A few days later, she sent another email:

> I'm sure you've already thought about the
> reactions of the LGBT, and the transgender
> community, in particular. Yes, you will get a fair
> amount of blowback for not hiring a transgender
> actor or actress to play the part of Maura. You
> will get a different kind of criticism for casting an
> actor who will probably never be able to "pass"—
> even if that fact raises other interesting questions
> about how we look at women, and transgender
> women in particular. The transgender community
> is rightfully crabby about having been portrayed
> in so many different wrong and insulting ways
> over the years, that it might never occur to them
> that anyone could ever do the story right. You
> saw my own initial reaction when you reached
> out to me with such gentleness and care. Anyway,
> having my name attached to your project will
> probably help some.

Jenny gave us all an assignment to read Julia Serano's book *Whipping Girl*. It's an amazing manifesto describing the complexities behind the hatred directed at trans women. Serano explains the assumptions underneath transmisogyny: some people think it's a *choice* to be trans, so only a crazy person would "choose" to give up all of that privilege. She also talks about how liberal feminists would rarely express disgust about cis women who didn't look "appropriate," but because they might still unconsciously think of trans women as men, it made it okay to make fun of them. It all turned my stomach.

Around this time, I remember watching a tall, skinny street kid, maybe drug addicted, a guy in his twenties, wandering around on Vermont wearing a sundress. He stood out on the street; everyone was looking at him. The same homeless kid, were they female but wearing a man's scruffy pants and shirt, wouldn't attract a second look. They might be exactly the same amount genderqueer, but the one who seemed to be male in women's clothing was alarming in the way a woman in men's clothing would not be. Realizing all of this was a rapid education and a giant awakening for me.

We all had a lot to learn. Jenny arrived at Honeycomb Hideout and wrote "FTM" (female to male) and "MTF" (male to female) on the board. These acronyms referred to people who were assigned the incorrect gender at birth. "Transgender" had recently come to replace "transsexual" as the correct way to refer to those folks. The word was mostly used to describe people who were making use of medical options like hormones and gender confirmation surgery to begin anew. These were the people we all understood to be trans.

The word "trans" is Latin for "bridge," she taught us next. Then she wrote the word "transbrella" on the whiteboard. "Not everyone is at one end of the spectrum or the other," she explained. People use the word *trans* to refer to all kinds of people, including drag queens, butch lesbians, and genderqueer folks, who metaphorically stand *on* the bridge, in the middle, rather than using it to cross from one side to the other.

As did cross-dressers.

Hmm. Cross-dressers. We had planned to move forward and tell the story of this family without invoking that group. Because cross-dressers were considered "part-time," they were often otherized by the queer community. Drag queens, who are also part-time, get a pass because their femininity is tweaked to perfection and used within the context of performance, celebration, art. But the mostly white, conservative men—those who were part of the Chi Chapter organization that Carrie had first pointed me toward—were pariahs. The way that they embodied the feared "man in a dress" image had been used as a weapon against the trans community. A right-winger could say, "So Jeffrey Tambor is pretending to be a woman on TV, but he's just pretending, so trans women are just pretending, right?"

All of this added up to a brand-new gigantic *oh, shit* moment.

This conflict came to life one night at a queer film festival called Outfest. They were screening the pilot. It's always so exciting for TV writers to get this kind of big-screen cinema moment. Most of us never experience audiences seeing our work. In those rare minutes in the darkened theater, the work projected on a grand scale, I finally felt less anxious. And so much gratitude.

The episode played. Afterward I took the stage with

most of the cast—Jeffrey Tambor, Gaby Hoffmann, Amy Landecker, Jay Duplass, plus Rhys and Zackary. We sat down to answer questions. The audience loved the show and hands shot up—they had so much to say.

Then an activist stood up and spoke. "I remember my relatives talking about blackface back in the day, where white men would dress up as black men, and it was very humiliating. We see your show as transface, you know."

My heart sunk.

My God, I hadn't been expecting this. I felt myself tearing up. *Hold it back,* I told myself, throat closing. I tried to answer: "I've been thinking about it constantly since I realized what it would mean to tell this story with Jeffrey," I responded. "I don't know if this helps, but I do believe it's possible that at the end of Maura's journey there might be a genderqueer identity there, as opposed to a trans woman identity."

Zackary Drucker spoke firmly but lovingly. "I think if we want to assassinate anybody who attempts to represent us, include us, employ us, we are making a huge mistake, we are shooting ourselves in the foot."

That thing happened when you don't cry from the first arrow but you do when someone defends you. Now tears flowed freely. I wiped them away.

The activist shot back at Zackary, "You are a paid apologist."

"Oh, please," Zackary said.

"And why are there only cis actors onstage? You're profiting off trans experience and trans pain," the activist added. She got up and left the theater.

I looked around. She had been right. There were no trans

actors onstage. We had added trans characters to the show now that we were writing the season, but the activist didn't know that; she had only seen the pilot. I expressed my hope that there would be other shows and more opportunities, but said that *this* was the show I was making, and I hoped that the conversations it dared to have would be helpful. Then I apologized.

We had *two* problems. One was that a man was playing a trans woman. It didn't matter that people would be more likely to find our show if they saw someone familiar transition—in this case the man who played the father on *Arrested Development*. The pilot probably wouldn't have been made starring someone without Jeffrey's stature.

The other problem was that the story we wanted to tell was about someone transitioning late in life who'd spent many years cross-dressing, maybe giving audiences the wrong message about transness. With Zackary, Rhys, and Jenny's help, we decided that, just to be safe, we should probably stay as far away from the idea of cross-dressing as possible. But as we began to hash out the backstory of a late-transitioning trans woman, it became clear that there was no way to get there without this aspect. What my parent was doing was what a lot of older cross-dressers were doing, and what Maura needed to do. She needed to start out in that community. We had a big whiteboard on the wall and we could see that there would be a climax around the revelation of Maura's time at Camp Camellia, a cross-dressing camp for closeted men. That would be our Season One journey.

Faith told us all about an actress she knew from Chicago named Alexandra Billings. We wanted to add a trans woman, and Davina was a name that spoke to the divine, to something holy. Her name went on the board. Over the next few months, using collaging and colored markers to create columns and gigantic grids, with many, many Post-its, we gave birth to the first season.

We sat on beanbags. I shared what I had learned from Joan about playable actions. We gathered around the idea that the audience sits in a chair at home, maybe even an easy chair, because they want their actual life to be easy. But for their entertainment, they crave *feeling* their protagonists *doing* something. Vigorously. Our ability to name the specific playable action of every character, whether it was for the whole series, a season, an episode, or a scene, became the mainstay of our technique. We asked ourselves questions like, *What does Maura want overall?* and *What does she want in this episode? What is Josh's deepest need and what is he doing to get what he wants in this scene?* The driving force of desire, what people want, and specifically, what they are doing to get what they want—was our North Star.

One of the writers had a friend with a genderqueer parent who used the name "Maddy" instead of "Daddy." We tossed around a few syllables until we came up with the name "Moppa." Kinda "Mom," kinda "Papa," a perfect made-up word for the Pfeffermans to use.

The next time I talked to Carrie on the phone, I gently used the word "Moppa" to see if it would stick. It did. She liked it. Faith started using it with her, too.

Even though we were holed up furiously writing, we still hadn't gotten the official word that Amazon was going to order the season. We felt a lot of confidence and love from them, we were all in it together, but they still needed to wait a few weeks to make the final decision after the pilot came out.

WHILE WE WAITED, I turned my attention back to my real family. It was time for Isaac to look at colleges, and so I planned an East Coast family excursion. Because Felix was only five, Bruce and I decided that, once there, we would take turns taking Isaac to schools. All four of us would be in the city for NYU and the New School, then I would take Isaac to Sarah Lawrence, Vassar, and Bard. Bruce and Felix would take the train up and we would switch kids, then Bruce would continue the rest of the road trip, hitting Wesleyan and Yale.

Any amateur marriage counselors playing along at home can see how asinine this plan was. Why didn't we do the whole thing as a family? Or, why didn't one of us just head east and do the whole tour alone with Isaac? I was trying so hard to be whatever I thought a good mom was.

Bruce and I were still in our chit-trading mode, taking turns parenting. We rarely all had dinner together. But what families really ate dinner together? None, I found out, which was why I wasn't as concerned as I should have been. That was something I learned about all families once you looked into it: that actually, no, no one really ate dinner together every night. This was everybody's family life, right? Switcheroo pods of two? It was usually me and Isaac together, and Bruce and Felix together.

Admin, planning, and the tweaking of itineraries stood in for normal conversations. Actual togetherness was minimal and always had the built-in release valve of when the switch would happen. The possibility of conflict made us agree on an imitation of peace.

Oh, ADMIN. I remember a time when Faith and her partner, Harlie, were first together. They would come to my house for a week and spend hours saying things like, "But if we leave at ten-fifteen we might not have as much walking-around time just us," which would get a response like, "Okay, so let's go at ten and then we'll have enough walking-around time just us before everyone else meets up with us at ten forty-five." *My God*, I thought, *go to your room for that kind of dirty talk.*

I have witnessed entire relationships that seem to wholly consist of admin talk. Ours was no different. Free-floating anxiety was replaced by the making of a neurotic and pre-cise diagram. I thought that the flow charts of *if this then that* would make a net, an intricate grid to insure us against having to handle a problem in real time.

It was a warm day in the fall when we all flew to New York and settled into a townhouse in Brooklyn. We had done a house swap with our nanny Galeit's sister and her family of four. As we were loading in, they were dragging their belongings into our house in L.A.

The next morning, we all went into the city to start the tours. As soon as Isaac saw the New School, he knew it was right for him. It was exactly what he was looking for, and every forum, every Q and every A, resonated *yes* for him. We did the NYU tour next, but the whole time Isaac let me know that he wasn't feeling it. Kids in gray hooded fleece pullover sweatshirts with big purple and white furry letters triggered him, as did anything that reeked of ice cream so-cials or semiformals. I had swallowed whole the messages from movies like *Animal House* and *Porky's*—that I had to experience the rah-rah aspects of college life to be a real student—but he looked askance at all that.

We still had a few colleges to see, so I rented a car the next day and we started up the Henry Hudson Parkway toward Sarah Lawrence for the first half of our planned itinerary. Isaac found Sarah Lawrence weird and culty and rural, Vassar too preppy and goyishe and rural, and Bard just too dang rural. This is a boy after my own heart. I'd raised him in Silver Lake to be a city boy. Nothing is scarier to city folk than a leafy lane in the pitch-black. The sound of an unseen animal cacawing in the distance, or even worse, pure silence, invokes sheer terror. It was only after I grew up and spent some formative years in the moist forests of Northern California that I learned to love the smells and sounds of nature, but Isaac didn't see the appeal.

We packed and repacked to head into the next leg of the trip. The town of Tivoli was booked, so we were in the nearby town of Red Hook, staying at the grossest little bed-and-breakfast we'd ever seen. It reeked of cinnamon potpourri and old musk and was crowded with dusty plastic houseplants and fake antique furniture. On the back porch, there was a cardboard box with dirty peeping chicks.

Isaac and I went downstairs to suffer through the group dinner that came with the room and then retreated to our quarters.

That night we had planned to see a film series at Bard, shorts by Miranda July and Ryan Trecartin. But when we got to the theater a few minutes late, expecting to have to crowd into seats in the back, we encountered a forlorn student wiping letters off the board. No one had shown up for the screening. We slinked away and back to the bed-and-breakfast.

"There's only one thing happening on any given night out here," he said.

"Maybe people are just busy," I said, hopeful.

He couldn't hold it in any longer: "I don't want to go to school in the country," he said. "I only want to be in New York, and I only want to go to the New School. College, for me, is just an excuse to live in New York."

Yup, he said that . . . one-hundred-percent comfortable with what came out of his mouth. I had to think fast. *So he wants to live in New York and major in Zabar's and Other Sandwiches. Dare I even add up the money we spent on private school? The tutors and the SAT test prep, the freelance college counselor? Should I push at least for a look at Wesleyan? See if the beautiful, crisp New England afternoons might grab his imagination? Gently explain to him about the teenage brain and neuroplasticity? Teach him that these days, we know that brains actually change shape—and that within the next year he might start loving biology or French philosophy or open meadows, and he might wish he could go deep into new areas without the distractions of being in the middle of Manhattan at Fourteenth and Sixth?*

What would a good mom do? I weighed the options. It was seven P.M. He was right; if we packed quickly we *could* ditch this corny B&B and be back in Brooklyn by nine-thirty that night and at Marlow and Sons the next morning for farm-to-table breakfast and cappuccinos. But I was wracked with indecisiveness. If this was a movie I was directing, I would be able to do it correctly. Tell people where to stand, what to say, and how to say it. But this wasn't a script, it was real life, and my son was asking for something with all of his heart and soul. He wanted to ditch. To walk backward off the diving board.

Was it my job to help him tolerate the urge to flee?

Probably.

Did I know that at the time? Nope.

"Fuck it," I said. "Let's hit the road."

It was dark on the Taconic State Parkway. Way too dark to be on such an unfamiliar road. My family has a thing against "driving at night." My mom is always telling any-one within striking distance that she's looking for a guy who can walk without a cane and drive at night. Driving at night is understood to be inherently dangerous, even at six-thirty P.M. in the summer.

Even worse than my fear about the enveloping night sky was the sinking feeling that I'd failed us. This was such a Soloway thing to do, to abandon the path without seeing it through to the end.

As Isaac and I sped down the pitch-black highway, optical-illusion rabbits leapt across the road at a full clip. My "everything happens for a reason" religion meant that if we were critically injured in a car accident that night it would be because of my poor parenting choices. A Ye Olde Russian *kina hora* evil eye made the span of time where we were changing plans based on a whim or my weakness dou-bly dangerous. Yup, *they died in a car accident because Jill is a bad mother and Jill is a bad mother because she worked all this admin out on her own and a good mother would be lovable and in a good marriage and they would have made these choices together, and honestly, does Bruce even want to do this part of parenting? Where he would help take charge of Isaac's future?*

Of course he doesn't, his actions have made that obvious, but Jill had to make giant administrative mega-plans to distract everyone from reality, and now look, Jill is parenting alone out here in upstate New York, broken, forever broken, so broken she had to come home from camp early and was now engendering that same essential brokenness, that lack of grit in Isaac. All because I didn't stay the course to Wesleyan.

My fingers gripped the wheel as I pretended to chat casually on the drive into the city. Isaac suggested a podcast: Elvis Mitchell interviewing David O. Russell about his filmmaking style. Isaac and I have exactly the same connection that I have with my sister Faith. We can feel each other's every blood pulse of anxiety, each carb craving and tummy ache. As I drove and we listened to Elvis and David O. have a mansplain-off, my mind wandered to all the ways that the "LET'S RUN!" feeling had chased me throughout my life.

There were so many original sin moments. Coming home from summer camp just three days into a six-week commitment. Impulsive trips in my early twenties to Europe and Israel and Costa Rica that were cut short by newer, stronger impulses to flee. A road trip with Johnny, when Isaac was still a baby, where we changed hotels a few times in one evening. Like a Jewish Bonnie and Clyde, we ran from imaginary villains like air-conditioning that smelled like cigarettes. What was I fleeing?

The way my anxiety works is a sort of OCD writ large. The obsessions and compulsions are not about touching doorways or counting cracks. Instead, there's a larger obsessive thought: *Cancel the second half of the road trip* or *I gotta leave camp* or *Why did I come to Costa Rica?* The obsessive part works like a pony walking in circles, my brain perseverating. When I'm in the middle of an obsessive tear, anything can get to me. I have to actively fight the compulsion to act on the obsessive thought.

My obsessive thoughts are the worst when I'm trying to make parenting decisions. It was really bad in the first few days after Felix started kindergarten. We were tortured about whether we had chosen the right school. While parking, I'd see a half-eaten burrito on a paper plate, beans everywhere, then start to worry for his pure, litter-free mind and decide we needed to switch to a private school. Then I'd walk into the building and see Felix get a hug and know deep in my heart that he was in the right place. Moments later a misspelled sign would cause me to lose faith in the administration. A mom I hadn't met with a haircut I wish I had quickly cemented the unwavering truth that these were my kind of people. And so on, back and forth and back and forth, all of the above happening within less than one minute.

A few months before the college trip, I'd taken to meditating and would proudly tell anyone who'd listen that I'd finally learned the difference between impulse and instinct. It's time, in case you were wondering. It's that simple. Let the back-and-forth go back and forth as much as you need to but don't make a quick decision. If you find yourself acting because you have to, and you have to *now*, don't. That's impulse. If the desire holds up over the course of the week or more, that's instinct.

After hours of driving in the dark, Isaac and I finally got back to Brooklyn. As we crossed the bridge, we played the Avett Brothers singing "I and Love and You" where they sang "Brooklyn, Brooklyn take me in" as an anthem.

We tromped up the five flights of stairs to our apartment swap. Bruce and Felix were halfway through an hour-long bedtime ritual. Both Bruce and I loved the feeling of lying down with Felix as he fell asleep, but this was getting out of hand. Whatever we should have done at a critical sleep-training juncture we most certainly hadn't.

Isaac and I dragged our luggage into the living room and raided the freezer as we waited for Bruce to come out. Finally, he did, but just to say *"Shush!"* and then go back in to stroke Felix's sweaty snoozing brow. No hero's welcome for us, no sirree.

That *you just know* feeling we'd had when Bruce and I met had faded away. It had given way to a million ways to fail each day. An interaction about what setting the toaster was on became a one-act play. Bruce and I were just trying to survive, in life and on this trip.

On that chilly Brooklyn night, as Bruce and I struggled to fall asleep in some other couple's lumpy bed, I thought about the show. We had just handed in the outline for a potential Season One. When we got back, we would hear Amazon's thoughts, and the pilot would be released. We'd know what the public thought, what critics thought. All I wanted to do was flee my real family and run into the arms of my fake family, the writers at the Honeycomb Hideout and the actors waiting to perform my version of reality.

I couldn't wait to get home.

ABOUT A MONTH or so after the New York trip, the pilot came out. I wasn't sure what to expect. I still had the question in my head of whether Amazon was actually a network or a channel. Would reviewers even notice? The writers and I prepared urgent emails and tweets that we would send to all our friends on the morning of the show's debut to get them to spread the word.

But a few hours after the pilot came out, we realized that the heavy lifting we thought we would have to do wasn't necessary. Within a day, a bunch of reviewers had posted their opinions.

They loved it.

Willa Paskin's headline at *Slate* was: "Amazon Has Finally Made Its *House of Cards*." *Vulture* called it the best pilot they'd seen in years. *HuffPo* said it was going to be the best new show of 2014. We were a mess of joy, dancing around the Honeycomb Hideout like fools.

A couple of days later Bruce and I were coming out of a parent-teacher conference at Felix's school when I got the call from Joe Lewis. "Why aren't you whooping?" Joe asked. "Because I'm on a street corner," I replied. "Well, do a little dance anyway," he said. I did. Bruce looked out the window and asked, "What are you doing?" I got in the car and told him. "We're going to series!"

We decided to have a party in the courtyard of our workspace. There was a scene in the pilot where Sarah talked about the Pupusa Lady at the Silver Lake Farmers Market. I'd written that moment as a shout-out to the real woman, whose name was Ruth. We catered in pupusas, Ruth set up the grill, and we threw buckets and buckets of fruit punch and vodka into giant dispensers, and blasted music.

Isaac and I walked up a side street to help Jeffrey find his way to the party. He wasn't really a Silver Lake person. It was like going to get Dad to bring him to our backyard where all of our friends were. Everyone was there—actors, friends of the show. More friends brought more friends. Zackary brought Van Barnes, a brassy blonde who was trans and lived in the Ozarks but wanted to move to L.A. to start a career in the TV business. At the end of the night, we were all leaning on the wall of the building, trying to come back down to earth. Van said the craziest things. She reminded me of my aunt Lily, whose catchphrase was "Close the door or you'll catch a cold in your vagina!" She was bawdy and raunchy and we all cracked the hell up, looking into the night sky at the future.

Yes. We were going to series. It was time to ramp up into full production mode. We said goodbye to the Honeycomb Hideout and moved to Paramount. On this grand old lot we found some crusty offices in the Hope Building that we loved. It seemed like the kind of place a detective would solve a cold case. There was even a dumbwaiter. We ran up and down the stairs like college kids claiming their rooms in a dorm.

Our production designer, Cat, began building the Pfefferman house on one of the giant stages. When she had first shown it to me on the scout as a possible pilot location, I just assumed we would always be going back to Pasadena to shoot. I couldn't believe we were actually building it. All over the Paramount lot, production offices were opening, people were making little laminated *Transparent* signs to put everywhere. Faith and I commandeered one of the golf carts and rode around the lot, hooting and singing made-up songs about golf carts and Hollywood.

But there were problems brewing out there. Just after the pilot was released, I went on Twitter to see what the trans activists were saying about it. They would love it, right? Wouldn't they all feel the way Jenny did? That the tenderness and nuance and art made up for the original sin of having cast a cis man?

The answer was no. They did not feel that way. In fact, a lot of them hated the show, and they hated me. Many tweeted they wouldn't even watch the pilot. They were full of anger. *Fuck*. We were writing a whole season that had Davina in it and so much other radical trans content, but they didn't know that yet.

I went to visit Zackary and Rhys in their office. How can it be that the continuing anger of the trans community keeps surprising me? The callouts and blowback were waking me up to the intensity of the issues that trans people face. Besides the physical danger in the world and the bathroom bills, there were tens of thousands of discriminatory laws on the books. This was a complicated community with diminished life options and no economic justice. At the root of their anger was a 41 percent attempted-suicide rate, and a disproportionate amount of homelessness and sex work. Violent crime. They struggled to get jobs, let alone jobs in Hollywood where they could make art out of their journey, as I had been lucky enough to do. I started to understand how things got worse when viewed through an intersectional lens. Many people of color, queer people, and trans people were dealing with multiple oppressions as well as class, which is not only a problem of money, but also of time, which is a problem for dreaming, for art making, and for voice. This creates major issues around representation. As a cis woman, I had felt so marginalized by cis men. I was beginning to confront my own truth—that I had been part of the problem, too, by only being a mentor for mostly cis white folk.

We created some guidelines to help shape the culture of the show. Inspired by Amazon's own leadership principles, we dubbed ours the "Topple Principles," named after our production company, and used them as guideposts for what we hoped to be about. We came up with seven of them:

1. OUR REVOLUTION MUST BE INTERSECTIONAL
   Lift up marginalized voices and use the power of story-telling to ignite an intersectional movement toward liberation.

2. BE CHILL
   No one is in trouble. No one throws anyone under the bus. Promote good vibes. Make grounded decisions. It's okay to move quickly, but if you're feeling under pressure try slowing down.

3. GATHER OFTEN
   Hold space for heart-connection. Get in a circle and check in with one another. Honor vulnerability and connect over gratitude.

4. KEEP THE MAMA WITH THE BABY
   Respect the creator's vision, intuition, and sparking of an idea. Keep them involved as long as possible.

5. BE BRAVE
   Ask: Has it been done before? Will it change the world?

6. THE PROCESS
   Beat changes are where the plot and story meet. Learn and speak the language of how action, beats, and beat changes generate blocking in scenes and movements in story.

7. PRINCIPLES OVER PRODUCT

We prioritize process that adheres to the above principles. We aim to foster collaboration and a spirit of generosity and abundance surrounding artistic vision.

Now that we had a series order, we had jobs to fill. We decided to institute something we called a Transfirmative Action Program. We were going to be sure that for any opening we could find on the show, we would submit trans or gender-nonconforming folk. Our goal was to hire at least one trans person within each department.

We created a spreadsheet with all of the people that Rhys and Zackary knew. Some had experience in Hollywood, some had adjunct careers that would help them succeed in the particular departments of television making. One by one, we went to every department head and asked them to interview particular people. We found a job for Van in set decoration—she'd had experience as a buyer for resale shops. The first day of production was getting closer. Any day now we would begin this giant experiment in inclusion, art making, and love.

7   BEAT CHANGE

I T WAS TIME TO START SHOOTING THE FIRST SEASON. FAITH MOVED
out of the Honeycomb Hideout and into our guest room.
It was fantastic to have her in the house, and for Felix
and Isaac to be able to spend time with their aunt. She was
always on the piano, making up songs. The house sounded
like our childhood home, silly improvised songs as our life's
wallpaper.

Ali, the queer poet who was now officially a TV writer,
found her own apartment with her girlfriend, Beth. We
cast Alexandra Billings as Davina, plus a few other main
characters for the first season. Carrie Brownstein was given
the role of Ali's best friend, Syd, and Melora Hardin played
Sarah's lover Tammy.

I called Joan, the acting guru who'd informed my process on *Afternoon Delight.* Could she work her magic again?
She agreed to create a series of workshops where we could
share her techniques with the actors and crew. Bruce and
I chose songs that represented each movement of the season. Working with Joan, the cast and crew did hours and
hours of grounding exercises, getting into our bodies like we

were back in high school drama class. We were developing a shared language.

We also graduated past the playable actions I'd understood and disseminated, and started to learn about something new: beat changes. A beat change occurs in the moment when a character attempts a new playable action in the process of trying to get what they want.

Joan insisted that a beat change happens for everyone in the room at the same time. Every actor, character, and crew member is connected to this agreed-upon moment of the beat change. She added that beat changes give birth to blocking, which means you let the beat changes tell you when and where to move, in the room, in the scene, in the episode, the season, or the series.

Laying the grid of beat changes on top of our playable actions was like finally learning music theory after years of playing the piano. It appealed to my sense of order and symmetry. I found so much simple joy spending time inside the beat change, the moment when emotion intensifies, necessarily giving birth to the next beat. It is *this* moment I want to slow down so that we can *get* it. As a director, it is the fish I have come for, and the camera is my net.

I loved the way this work created boundaries around a particular emotional experience. I had to feel things in order to do the job. I don't like feeling things. I'm not good at it. But this way of working was forcing me to feel things.

On the set, we would all lean over the open hood of a script with the beat changes mapped out. Is the actual change the moment when a character says, "Can I tell you something?" Or when the other person looks up, realizing this is about to be something good, or bad? Is it the nod of consent, *Yes, tell me,* or is it the first breath that says, "Here I go"? I spoke about the nuances of beat changes with the editors, too. Sometimes during post-production, I'd encourage everyone to take off their shoes and stand in the editing bay, planting our feet into the flat gray carpet, to see if we could feel the beat changes in our lower bellies.

IN FALL 2014, we were finally ready to premiere the first season of *Transparent.* Amazon commandeered a gigantic theater that holds 1,200 people downtown at the Ace Hotel. It was one of those enormous life moments that felt like cracking through the sound barrier. Every queer person in L.A. was there. More friends than we knew we had. A bunch of famous people.

I gave an opening speech, then went down to the basement to smoke a joint with Joe Lewis, then took my seat and settled in to watch the first three episodes in this giant cavern of joy.

I sat next to Bruce, along with his parents and his aunt and uncle, all of us a proud delegation in the center of the theater. My mom was a few rows over and two rows back on the right, with Faith and Isaac. Carrie was on the left, with Zackary and Rhys. Even the Great Ellen Silverstein was there, a few rows back.

Later she would ask me why Bruce's extended family had pole position in the center of the room and the Soloways were scattered around the theater.

"Oh, was it like that?" I asked.

"Yes."

"Ah, I guess I would have been too anxious to sit with my mom or Moppa," I said.

That night, after I was sure our parents were off to bed in their hotel rooms, Faith and I went up to the Ace Hotel rooftop to celebrate with everyone. I couldn't find Bruce. I texted him—he wanted to go home. That was fine. Word was that Tegan and Sara were chilling on the rooftop. I also noticed that my new friend Mel was there.

I had met Mel a few weeks before at an event called Lez Bowl. It was at Shatto 39 Lanes, a weird vintage bowling alley in Koreatown. The evening was a full dyke takeover thrown by two women, Cass Bugge and Molly Schiot. They were deeply in love in that doppelbanger way. Both looked like mini Carrie Brownsteins and seemed on Instagram to be deeply crazy about each other, to have the ideal relationship. Like, *We've found love, so let's celebrate by putting on a lezzie night for the world at the bowling alley. Let's design the flyer! Let's send it out together!*

As we all took over the bowling alley, the sheer variety of the ways to be queer and alive in Los Angeles in 2014 exploded my mind. There were high-femme chicks in bright red lipstick and halter tops and low-femme women in bell bottoms and neither-here-nor-there gender mediums. And there was a pack of really butch dudes who moved like greasers—the kind that would normally trigger me, guys leaning on each other, whispering about the chicks.

But these guys were girls. They were feminist humans, which meant we would actually have a lot in common, and one of them, Mel, looked really familiar the first time I saw her. She was wearing a vintage French fisherman's jacket and matching cap—which somehow communicated a kind of Midwestern Grandpa chic. Mel actually *was* from Chicago, from Skokie. That was where our family had gone to my aunt Ruth's house every Sunday, where we'd sit in the basement and watch my uncle Howard's slide shows. Mel and I made a bunch of inside jokes, talked about the menu at Barnum and Bagel and which kind of pickles we preferred.

Bruce had gone home and to bed early, so Mel and I rolled together. Beat change. Afterward, I went home and googled her, and then a few nights later invited her to a shared birthday party Amy Landecker and I were throwing. It was at a downtown nightclub with disco floors that lit up in colored blocks. Everyone shoved into the space and we danced our hearts out. Kathryn Hahn was there, too.

Kathryn had joined the cast midseason. The tragic passing of Philip Seymour Hoffman brought her Showtime series to an end after the first season. I wrote the part of Rabbi Raquel quickly, just for her. By episode five, she shows up and changes everything, with her outsider, spiritual gaze on this family. I couldn't believe I got to have my sweet buddy and muse share in this amazing experience with us on the show.

As I danced with Mel and Kathryn and Amy Poehler, who had joined us, I tried to push down the anger that Bruce hadn't yet arrived to my birthday party. Felix was having a tantrum that night. I'd asked Bruce to let the sitter handle it, and he'd said the sitter couldn't handle it, and so I'd taken an Uber to the party alone.

I'd wanted him to come with me.

I should have said, "Babe. It's my birthday. Felix will be fine, we got this."

Instead, I thought, *I can't believe he doesn't know that I*

need him to come with me now rather than meet me there later.
I can't believe this is the person to whom I will be married for
the rest of my life. I don't want to tell him the ways I need him.
I want him to know.

Instead I'd breezily called out, "All good!"

He said he'd come later once Felix was asleep. He ended
up getting there late and leaving early.

AFTER MY PARENT came out, the intensity of my own gender
issues started to make more sense. And by gender issues, I
mean that the things I imagined felt easy to most women
felt impossible to me. When I took the time to get dressed
up for a night out, I would fly into a seethe that would become a hissing rage if Bruce's first words when he saw me
were not "You look beautiful."

"WHY DIDN'T YOU SAY I LOOK BEAUTIFUL?!"

"You look beautiful. I'm saying it right now!"

"But you didn't say it when you saw me. You asked me
something about what shelf the fitted sheets go on."

"Exactly, I was distracted. You look beautiful."

(Crying now.) "That's all I ever need: for the person I
love to see me and say I look beautiful."

"Don't give me orders. I need a second; I'm a human
being."

"It's not an order—this is sad, I am sad, why can't you
see that?"

"Don't get all dramatic now."

"See how withholding you are?"

"Don't label me."

"You're labeling me a label maker."

"You're the label maker."

I wasn't sure why dressing up made me so upset. I guess "fancy" became a time where I couldn't get away with my boyish, not-trying uniform of jeans and T-shirts. Dressing up meant dressing femme. "Date night" became code for "We're going to have a fight in three hours." When Bruce and I finally faced each other, we did so with one hand on our pistols.

BRUCE'S BEST FRIEND was an eternal bachelor who had a thing for looking at real estate. Bruce helped him find a house a block away from us and he moved in before I knew it was even happening.

"Why didn't you tell me he was moving onto our street?" I asked.

"I didn't think you'd care," he answered.

Each day would end with Bruce going down the street to chill at his best friend's house. Dip in the pool. Sometimes taking Felix. I handled my anger by hanging out with all my new dyke friends. Mel had a girlfriend named Eden, and I invited them both to hang out. Their friends came over. Soon our backyard was full of women. After years of living and working with only men and boys, I had queer people around everywhere. I loved it.

Mel and Eden became Bruce's and my new favorite couple. Throughout our marriage we'd had people like this in our lives—the new twosome we couldn't live without, Jonah and Michaela, Mark and Cerise, Micah and Liba. We were always happily homosocial. Bruce bonded with his boys; I had my girls. But I imagined we were behaving in a manner that saluted the Armenian families I would see on my walks home in Los Feliz. After dinner, the men go out on the front porch to smoke cigars and talk sports while the women gather in the kitchen, lit up talking.

Hanging out with a dyke couple instead of a straight couple changed things. We weren't sure who belonged to whom, who were the men, who were the women. Before long, Mel and I started making plans to see each other outside of the foursome. Each morning after I exercised, she and I would get on the phone, talking about the billion things we were both thinking. We had revolution on our minds, crazy planet-destroying thoughts about how to topple the patriarchy. Messiah-pariah complexes, a love for attention, a love for new words and ideas that were slightly newer than yesterday's.

I told my old best friends I had a new best friend. Soon they got mad when I said Mel's name, said *ugh, not* her *again.* Bruce felt it, too. He started to feel like maybe I was calling her during the day to check in about every little feeling instead of doing that with him. What did you have for lunch? Club sandwich. What about you? Haven't eaten yet.

There was some notion of polyamory floating around in our midst. The word was that all of the parents at a school in Echo Park were switching partners and it was fine. People hear what they want to hear. I brought home the book *The Ethical Slut,* a guide to open relationships. Bruce didn't want to read it. Maybe he knew that trying out poly is not the thing to do at the moment your marriage is falling apart.

He told me to stop seeing Mel. Instead, I kissed her. I instantly knew, *Oh, I'm queer, and wow, okay, so this is about something else.*

A million ideas came to me about the ways in which every single move my body had ever made when it came to sex had actually been subtly meant to perform something for men.

What did I really want? I was going to find out.

Kissing Mel and having sex with Mel and loving Mel spiraled my mind and body into a tornado. We can do anything. Everything. I looked back at the past thirty years, being the kind of straight woman who would crunch up my nose and say *ew* when talking about vaginas. That faux disgust, maybe born of being raised in this misogynist world. When people ask me about how you switch from dick to pussy, I remind them, it all seems gross in the abstract, and then in reality you fall in love and all you want is all of that person's body, every last bit.

Maggie Nelson unpacked the idea of women loving one another as you wish to be loved in *The Argonauts* when she said: "an encounter with sameness . . . can be important as it has to do with seeing reflected that thing which has been reviled, with exchanging alienation or internalized revulsion for desire and care. To devote yourself to someone else's pussy can be a means of devoting yourself to your own."

I was an adolescent anew with Mel. When I was with Bruce I had somehow become an older woman, an adult resigned to this mostly disconnected thing in exchange for the idea of *But look at our beautiful family.* Never mind that I would never have good sex in a new way ever again. Okay. That's marriage. I had accepted the bargain.

Was I meeting a new part of myself? Was all of this about Mel? It didn't matter. Risk, and the willingness to be hurt, sent me hurtling toward her. I wanted to go after her, go toward her, make things for her, make her happy. Everything was happening way too fast. The not being able to stop. The undertow that pulls you away from the shore.

I fell in love with Mel, and I fell in love with being the person who was doing the doing. Holy shit, my whole life, I had been the person waiting for the guy to initiate, or at least the person trying to do what might make him do the thing I wanted. What did it mean now that there was a world of women, queer women, who, besides wanting me, might even want to know what I wanted?

Following the want was going to explode our house. Ignoring the want was going to explode me.

I offered up the notion of bird nesting to Bruce. "Let's take turns in the house," I said. "Week on, week off. Take some time to understand what is happening." He didn't want that. He quickly moved out, found a divorce lawyer, and put a custody schedule in place.

A FEW WEEKS LATER, *Transparent* was nominated for a Golden Globe. The day it was announced, we were all at work. The hundred or so people on the set let out a huge whoop. News crews came to interview us at lunch: *How does it feel?* We had never even bothered to imagine that this was in the realm of possibility. Joe Lewis put his arm around me.

"Everything's going to change," he said. "We're going to look back on this time and think about how good it all was."

Before all of this, Bruce was going to go to the Golden Globes with me. But he was so furious that he didn't even want to be in L.A. He took Felix snowboarding.

I was so scared to be facing all of this alone. We were

between seasons so Faith was back in Boston. I called and asked her to fly out to L.A. to be with me. She landed and came to the same hotel in Santa Monica where we had first made up Maura. The cast was staying there and we were getting ready for the big day.

Faith and I had breakfast at a table overlooking a palm-frondy courtyard.

"What if you and I are the parents now?" I asked her. We decided that, yes, we could be the new parents, and our three children would be our children. Our twosome was the North Star of my family now. We had a *Grey Gardens* spiritual sister handshake.

With Faith next to me I can do anything. She is actual liquid faith. When she is near me I'm okay and nothing else matters. Two decades ago we moved to separate cities because we knew how hard it would be to form bonds with other people that were as deep. We'd had marriages and children and yet now we were here again, the only ones we could really depend on.

ALL OF THE ACTORS from the show packed into SUVs and we rode in caravan to the Beverly Hilton. Walked the red carpet. I had been getting to know the press corps, and they had been getting to know me.

"Hey, Jill," one of the photographers said to me as I posed, "you're not a hand-on-your-hip kind of a girl."

She saw through my awkwardness, the fake femme thing I had been doing for the past year as I got used to being photographed.

"Oops," I said. "I'm sorry." I was embarrassed that I was getting it wrong.

"No," she said, "just have fun. You're doing great. Just don't do that thing where your hand is on your hip."

Instead I made serious faces and gave birth to a Power Rangers stance with legs spread wide.

We moved as a group during the pre-party with sponsored drinks. Then we all went into the huge ballroom, tight with our new family, which included Jeff Bezos, who I'd met before, and who was delightful and admiring. We sat at the round table, tried to eat the meal, but were too nervous.

"And for Best Comedy...*Transparent*!" The theme music started playing, we all jumped up, and the world swelled.

Then time slowed down, and as we walked past the tables surrounding us, I saw every single executive who'd passed on the show when I pitched it.

We piled onto the stage. I loved what I was wearing. A perfect sky and royal blue Kenzo suit and platform Prada creepers, instead of the ball gowns we were expected to wear. Oprah watched as I accepted that big marble statue with a golden world on top. I had my speech memorized, about a teenage trans girl named Leelah Alcorn, who had recently taken her own life. Then I dedicated the award to my moppa and said: "Thank you for coming out because in doing so you made a break for freedom, you told your truth, you taught me how to tell my truth and to make this show. And maybe we're going to be able to teach the world something about authenticity and truth and love. To love."

8   CRACKING OPEN

M EL AND I FELL INTO A CREATIVE EXPLOSION AS WE FELL IN LOVE, something I've learned is pretty common with girls. We started a project with the most innocent of intentions when we were just buddies—a comedic short film about how to make women ejaculate. I would direct and Mel would be the lead, taking us on a tour of a supersized vagina while wearing rain gear.

Making art with Mel was like making art with Faith, or with Hahn and all my other muses. You get in a room with people you love and make one another laugh while attempting to capture the feeling of it. While researching our project, Mel and I became pure zealots when we encountered the lack of information about the size and shape of clits. It is not actually the thing that occasionally pokes out of the hood! It is something the size and shape of squid, and it moves through the labia, into the thighs and back toward the G-spot. This is like having a word only for the tip of a dick and not also one for the shaft. So that whole debate—is it this kind or that kind of an orgasm, vaginal or clitoral?—it turns out: IT'S ALL ONE THING.

We honestly couldn't believe that this information had

been kept from us, that women have this extended organ inside of them, which we nicknamed the VCVC, the Vaginal Clitoral Vulval Complex. The theory of our video was about wholeness and female pleasure as the key to worldwide revolution: if and only if Mel could make millions of gallons of female ejaculate rain across the planet, Father Patriarchy would be drowned in the flood and peace would reign.

The production and costume department heads from *Transparent* helped us out—Cat built the giant vagina and Marie did the costumes. It was so silly, our collective co-delusion. A folie à deux. With all of that mixed up with falling in love, I felt every part of me ballooning. I just couldn't wait to get in the same room as Mel. To do it all. Kiss and have sex and make things. We were coming alive together and making a film about coming, zero fucks given. There was no money in it, just pure delight.

Obviously, our shared delight did not delight Bruce. He wasn't speaking to me, and asked his family to please let me know I was disinvited to his niece's bat mitzvah. I was hurt until I remembered that I'd started making a female ejaculation video with my new lover.

I had empathy for Bruce. I knew he must have been feeling the energy of Mel and me out there in the world, seeing us together on Instagram. It was so weird; I had never seen him in any way vulnerable before this moment. I was shocked when I saw him falling apart; he was unrecognizable. I kept doing the math: you seemed to really dislike me when we lived together, so what exactly is the size of this pain? That was always my job, to display the pain or be in pain, and it was his job to say I was making too big a deal of things.

Our breakup coincided with another catastrophe in his family. Moments after the bat mitzvah I missed, Bruce's older sister, Tracy, announced she was leaving her husband. They had two daughters and a house that we had loved to go to for holidays, it was our family history home, but now it was over for them, too. This beautiful extended family, Bruce's parents with their gorgeous South African dignity, their boundaries and belief in *family first*, it was so sad seeing them experiencing a shattering of a full two-thirds of our world.

Even though Mel and I had both hurt people, we wanted to believe we could pull out receipts that said we never did anything until we were officially single. Intrigue, flirting, intimacy, all of it was happening while I was with Bruce, so he despised her. It was obvious that if I would just break up with Mel, things would calm down. But I couldn't, life was *Us* starring *Us*, and every day involved activities—an elaborate secret mission to a spy shop or climbing to the top of Griffith Park, the obligatory instigation of a Dropbox folder where we would share pages and pages and pages of poetry. I was so distracted that I ran out of gas in my car for the first time in my life. I'm not the kind of person who lets it even dip below halfway.

Bruce kept popping out from around a corner just at the moment we would kiss goodbye. At one point it became clear that if we continued at that rev rate it would result in a restraining order or a dog bite.

The video we made was called *If You Build It She Will Come*, and we had a massive release party at the Eagle, a grimy leather bar in Silver Lake. Every lesbian we had ever met was in the room. But now that both of our partners (and everyone else in our lives) knew that we were a couple, the manic energy—our love story forged in the fire of a new idealized self—fizzled. We immediately transitioned into being friends—another thing I found out lesbians are really good at.

A FEW WEEKS LATER, my therapist, Ellen, called. She wanted to change our therapy time, which was unusual. I got into my car and headed to Beverly Hills.

When I walked in, she was standing instead of sitting.

She said it quickly, as if that was the only way to say it.

"Jill, I have cancer."

I sat down.

She had been diagnosed with pancreatic cancer. The worst fucking cancer. The cancer that takes people down in four months, as I had just seen with my friend's dad.

We stared into each other's eyes.

What can I say? Can I say all the things you're not allowed to say in therapy? Are you allowed to lift your boundaries if your therapist has terminal cancer? Could I drive her to chemo and then sit at her feet, pick her up and hold her in both of my arms in a fireman's carry? Kiss her forehead?

My heart pounded. This wasn't okay.

I asked her what the symptoms were.

Pain below the stomach that she had thought was a muscle pull.

How long had she known?

Just a week or so.

"I can't live without you," I said.

"It's not a death sentence anymore, pancreatic cancer, I'm not going anywhere," she promised.

I tried to do therapy like it was a normal day, but I was on a dual track, experiencing the crazy spinning feeling of a nightmare I'd always imagined, a clock ticking down. What if you only had a few hours with someone before they died? How would you spend it? And if you spent even one of those seconds wondering how much time you had left, did it mean that you weren't getting it right?

What was this obsession with getting things right? This OH GOD, IT FINALLY HAPPENED feeling. I thought about the way that my mother has always been preparing herself for the deadly five-car crash behind every phone ring. The day I gave birth to Isaac. Even though they were divorced, my parents got in the same room to wait for news. They were impatient, and when Faith didn't answer their calls, they called the hospital. The nurse who picked up the phone told them that I couldn't speak to them then. My mom became certain I'd died in childbirth and the new baby had died as well.

"OH MY GOD, WHAT IS WRONG?" my mom asked when Faith finally called her back.

"Nothing," Faith said. "Jill's great, the baby's great, why?!" My mom sighed tears of relief. Faith promised her that I was alive and the baby was alive and all was well. His name was Isaac, and he was eight pounds and fifteen ounces and perfect.

"WHY DO YOU think I'm running so fast?" I asked Ellen.

"Maybe we're all trying to feel complete," she said. "We

have these missing pieces. Babies are naturally dependent on people. They're really just these love-seeking things, but it's only through the kindness of our parents meeting our needs that we are actually alive. So we constantly read them for signals that they're going to protect us. We learn as we become children that there are parts of us that are acceptable and parts of us that are not. Besides learning language, we learn a language of how to be. We take those parts of ourselves that make us less likely to be loved by our parents and we put them into a bag and hurl them out into the world."

"That's so sad," I said.

"But that's what life is," she said. "A process of finding your bags. If you meet someone who has one, you have a strong reaction. You might really love or really hate or be attracted to that person who is holding one of your bags. You have to understand what parts of yourself you gave away."

Gosh.

Was there really enough time left?

We hugged. She said she was switching to office hours at her house in Santa Monica. Would I be able to make the drive?

Of course, I said.

BRUCE AND I were already in divorce proceedings, but it didn't matter, he was still my first call from the car. Then I told my mom. They were sweet and sympathetic. But talking to them didn't help. Nobody would ever understand how much I needed Ellen. I got home and unraveled, pounding on my computer keyboard like it was a piano, begging the great beyond to help.

I wanted to get Ellen's directive right. What had I jettisoned? What did I have to do to be loved? I couldn't blame my parents for anything. I can barely get through a day of parenting; I'd bet they probably didn't know how to get through a day either, let alone have the distance to stand back, assess us, see if we had all our parts.

I had hurled myself so quickly toward Mel, and away from this thing called family—family that I had made in the hopes that I would stop running—but it hadn't worked. What did Bruce hold in his bag that I had gotten rid of? What did Mel hold in hers?

I thought about the Pfeffermans and the glowing ring of mystery that holds them together. In the center of the spinning ride, there is a magnet that pulls and pushes simultaneously. It's like everyone's afraid to see what's in the middle. My writing went in spirals and so did I. None of it added up. I finally turned off my computer, wondering if I could please quickly find a new hobby, a hobby that wasn't writing about shame.

WE WENT BACK to the writers' room to hatch Season Two. Over the summer we'd put even more effort into finding more trans people. We found Silas Howard and had him join as a director. We hired Our Lady J to join the writers' room. I'd met her a few years previously at the GLAAD awards. She was a composer and pianist and performer and hadn't written for TV yet, but she submitted a beautiful short story about growing up trans in a Mennonite community in Pennsylvania. Her first week of work we all took a glamping writers' retreat to El Capitan and sat in circles and talked through our dreams for ourselves and the characters. We had a shaman come. She did magic incantations as we lay on the floor of a yurt and asked the souls of the Pfeffermans to tell us what they wanted to do.

Having Lady J on the staff transformed things. It was impossible to believe that we had written the show for an entire year without any transfeminine gaze in the room. I realized how awful it was that we hadn't put in more effort sooner. With Lady J there, Maura's story line started to come alive. We could now really tell a story about Maura dating and longing and thinking about surgery and medicine and friendships, and what it felt like to be in the world as a trans woman.

As Lady J talked about her childhood, we began to build a world out of Maura's family history. Her mother, Rose, and how they all emigrated from Poland and Russia. Henry Winkler came to visit the writers' room and brought us a beautiful spider plant, the kind with babies that drop from it on green strands. "This plant was made from the cutting of another plant that traveled here in the foot of a casket," he told us. "My mother snuck the plant in the night they left Germany in a hurry. Hiding things wherever they could. You can have it for your writers' room." He told us about hiding precious family heirlooms inside of melted chocolate that hardened in time for transit. We asked if we could write it into the show.

My own moppa had ideas, too. Our relationship had improved; we'd gotten closer. We were past the big revelation of transness, and she loved the show and the way it was holding space for a new reality for all of us. We got into the fun of thinking and dreaming together. She emailed me an article about Magnus Hirschfeld, and I passed it around to the writers.

Hirschfeld was a Jewish sexologist in pre-Holocaust Germany who had started the Institut für Sexualwissenschaft, a museum of sexual and gender exploration and a haven for queer people of all bodies and sexualities in 1930s Europe. We all lit up with possibilities. Maybe we could set Maura's family's story near there? What if Grandma Rose had a trans sister? We named her Gittel and started to channel the story.

Ali Liebegott wanted to re-create Michfest, also known as the Michigan Womyn's Music Festival, a weeklong feminist Woodstock. The festival was probably folding soon, under attack by activists and trans folk for insisting that the space was only for "women-born women." We talked and imagineered and dreamt until we found a way to weave the Black Forest of Germany into the green valleys of the Midwest. Could our characters time travel? Why not?

We wrote a huge wedding as a season opener where the eldest Pfefferman, Sarah, would commit to her new lesbian lover, Tammy. Except something went wrong during the ceremony, some weird epigenetic timer went off. When Sarah watched Tammy dance with her WASPy tanned sailboating father, she felt somehow broken and unable to be loved. Her clarity about what was wrong with her and in the relationship crystallized. We created a moment out of her brokenness that opened up a wormhole from her wedding's dance floor into a parallel dance floor at the institute where 1930s queer people were getting their vibe on, cabaret-style.

We dove into each character's past, including Maura reimagining a could-have-been childhood with her new friends Davina and a third lead character we added, Shea, played by Trace Lysette. Trace was new to Hollywood and had auditioned for the role of Davina the previous year. Before she transitioned she had come from the world of drag balls and queer family. We were blown away by her artistic potential and started to think about a story for her in Season Three as Josh's love interest.

We also decided that Ali's character needed to go back to college and that she should be a gender studies TA. I could feel all of my loneliness and longing superimposed onto Ali. All of my fear of losing those I loved, of losing Ellen.

"Ali needs real love," I said.

"Maybe she falls in love with her professor," Bridget offered.

"The professor should be like Eileen Myles," Ali Liebegott said.

We all googled this great American dyke artist wanderer poet. We watched her read some of her poems on YouTube. She had an amazing Boston accent.

"Perfect," I said. "The character has to be just like her."

"YES!" Faith screamed. "Cherry Jones! We have to get Cherry Jones to play her!"

That night when I got home, my friend Sarah Gubbins, a playwright from Chicago who had just moved to L.A., came by to give me a book. It was Chris Kraus's *I Love Dick*. I opened it and saw that this very same Eileen Myles had written the foreword. I inhaled her reckless prose:

> Chris's ultimate achievement is philosophical. She's turned female abjection inside out and aimed it at a man. As if her decades of experience were both a

> *painting and a weapon . . . thus when* I Love Dick
> *came into existence a new kind of female life did too.*
> *By writing a total exegesis of a passion, false or true,*
> *she is escorting the new reader into that world with her.*

The way Eileen named sexual obsession and abjection not as spinning loss but instead as the essential shape of the female voice was so beautiful. Her words pulled me into a heroic idea of going down a drain actively—winning by drowning, by allowing. Anointing that angry empty internal nothingness with the forward-moving power to express every want in each paragraph.

I grabbed a Lydia Davis book off my shelf and flipped through to a passage I had marked:

> *I find it fairly easy to be nothing in the morning but by late afternoon what is in me that is something starts throwing its weight around. This happens many days. By evening, I'm full of something and it's often something nasty and pushy.*

I saw how my manageable mornings gave way to ugly nights. A pattern I had laid onto my life. The morning of my life had been heterosexual and according to plan, and now the afternoon and the evening were getting queer and problematic, and it all felt so scary, and also somehow very much my story.

Chris Kraus and Eileen Myles and Lydia Davis's idea of the Female Monster lit me up, and I kept grabbing books, until I found an old one of Eileen's that I owned but somehow hadn't yet read: *Chelsea Girls.*

I opened it and lost my mind remembering something I never got the chance to learn. This monstrous chasm-on-chasm love and how it fuels a kind of lust that can be thought of as queerness.

I looked at my calendar and realized that I had a panel coming up in San Francisco with Eileen. This is what's wrong with writing a TV show about people who are all fragments of you. You can never tell what comes first, the fiction or the reality.

I asked Ali for Eileen's phone number, ostensibly to discuss a possible after-party where our various friends could repair for a cocktail after the show. Where would she be staying? She said she'd be at the Phoenix Hotel. I would be at the W. We tried to come up with a good in-between place.

A few weeks later I flew to San Francisco for the panel. In my mind I was already Ali, the character, ready to fall in love with her professor. *Inside voice,* I reminded myself. *Get out of your mind and into your body. None of this is real, calm down.* So why was my heart beating so hard when I got to the stage door to do the sound check, and saw Eileen there? I recognized her, but it took her a moment to recognize me.

"Oh, hi, I'm Jill," I said, self-conscious in my poufy red jacket and boots with thick heels.

"Yeah," she said, and we had an awkward shuffle, a do-si-do as we tried to figure out where to stand.

We spent about a half hour or so in the green room where I mostly avoided her. I tried to steal looks at her while we were onstage—Michelle Tea and Eileen and me. The host of the event investigated the theme of the evening, the idea of the imagined audience when you *tap tap tap* on the computer, by asking us:

Who do you write for?

I said that sometimes I wrote for my sister, Faith, and sometimes I wrote for Michelle Tea. Michelle Tea said she wrote for Eileen. Eileen said, "Oh, myself and the people attracted to that vision, I guess. Also the people I'm already talking to in my head, but like the weather they are always changing."

My breath caught in my throat. Her brain.

The host then asked us to talk about the books we loved that we'd brought to donate to the museum. I brought one of Michelle's books and Michelle brought one of Eileen's and Eileen brought the book *Masochism* by Gilles Deleuze.

I wondered what it would feel like to be in love with Eileen and what it would mean if this hero with the gigantic mind could be my new imaginary reader for everything I would ever write again. My artist's voice could become a devotional act instead of a moneymaking one. What would it mean to fall in love with the mind you are writing for as you are becoming yourself? Even imagining that she might never love me back felt desperate but good. This new feeling of risk with women felt like something opening instead of something doomed.

We all went to a bar afterward. A Dutch girl in her twenties was hanging around. I had heard that Eileen dated only really young women. I was fifty but felt fifteen. I shooed the Dutch girl away with weird possessive looks. Finally, everyone left the bar.

Eileen and I laughed as we watched businessmen try to pick up women, and then went outside and took multiple laps around the block. That feeling before the first kiss. All of the desire expanding inside of you, that *I can't wait to kiss / but this feeling of wanting to kiss / is better than anything that can come after it / I'll always want to be in this feeling.*

We kissed on a really unromantic street in San Francisco that was really romantic anyway. The mutual surrender into the unknown. That floating seesaw of the two of us in that space between up and down. No one is in charge, just this love thing hovering that calls us in.

She invited me back to her hotel room but I was too scared. When I thought about myself being seen by her, I became concerned that I was wearing the wrong bra.

The next morning, I realized that she could be a real match. She didn't work on the TV show. She wasn't in a relationship with anyone else. Maybe this could be something. We made plans to see each other in New York.

9 MAKING HISTORY

GOT HOME FROM SAN FRANCISCO AND ORDERED ALL OF EILEEN'S
books. I stacked *Maxfield Parrish* on top of *Inferno* on top
of *Snowflake / different streets*, alternating between reading her stuff and writing my own, getting hot in the neck
and forehead. One sentence about how she writes drove
me bananas. It was about how she goes out and dares the
city to force poems out of her, how she experiences life and
waits for the gusts. The way her voice moved, it was so sure
of itself and so sure of queerness, describing wanting the
highs and the lows, the sky and the weird little restaurants
and animals and pussies and fucking and women and girls,
and how that want had felt for decades. That's me trying
to write like her. Her words were more like: *The ocean / is
a feast / & it's here / I bring my / water tree book / feet, taste.*

I was six months into queerness. I wanted to mainline.

We talked on the phone every night. She sent me the
galley for her new collection of poetry and I read her poems
back to her in funny character voices. I can do a really
spot-on old southern civil servant gentleman, a crusty slow-
talking conservative, and he sounded really funny slogging
his way through her words, which were meant to be read

from sweaty woman to sweaty woman. Together we imagined this man accidentally picking the wrong book off the shelf at the library and doing a stilted reading to astonished patrons:

When I read books I think of my cunt. If it's about love of God, the hotter I get.

Then I'd flip, phone book–style, to another page and keep reading oh-so-slowly in that man's voice:

Oh Love, I love you so much. The crying babies of the sirens pass through the town, I am expected to do more and more and more.

I wrapped myself in her inside-out shame—open, open, open—then got on an airplane and went to New York.

RIGHT AFTER WE WON the Golden Globes for *Transparent*, Amazon began to pour a lot more money into promotion. We were thrilled. It felt like people in the world were starting to know about the show—this show that began as this little private thing I wrote to hold my emotions, becoming slightly larger when the cast and crew joined in, and then even larger when the first season aired. But now there was a giant marketing spend. The show was exploding. While we finished writing Season Two, we were doing a bunch of press and public screenings. I did my first junket, going up and down hotel hallways into rooms with different arrangements of reporters and actors. Roundtables. Journalists from Europe.

Eileen came to a big screening at the Paley Center. Afterward, we got in a hulking black SUV that was waiting outside, and escaped to my room at the Bowery Hotel and had sex for the first time. She knew that she knew every-thing about being queer and I knew nothing, so there was a lot of clarity around the dynamic. Or, as the kids might say, it was *on*.

The next morning, I ordered room service and she made a joke that after I signed the bill I should point to her in the bed and calmly say, "Oh, this was in my bed when I got in the room. I wonder what it is."

We laughed and laughed for days. Life back in my belly, legs vibrating, everything alive. We walked the streets of the East Village and went to hang at her apartment, which might have been like the Tenement Museum except it was the Poet Museum, where her life has been preserved in amber, or maybe in dust, for the forty years she's lived there. She was Kerouac and I was a groupie and I wasn't sure if I could even sleep over—was that dog food on the bed? No red flags—she was Eileen Myles, so everything was special and not weird, or if it was weird that made it more special. Love means you allow that person to be anything, right?

"There is a character based on you," I had to keep saying in my head before I actually said it to her aloud. *How will this sound?* The more time that passed the more I realized I'd have to account not just for the original lie but also for the length of time where I kept it from her.

"There is a character based on you, but it's not you, of course, just like Ali isn't me. But some people will probably think it is you."

She thought about it for a few minutes, then decided she didn't care. For decades, Eileen had been writing poems about people she loved and had to defend her right to do so. She wasn't mad, and she also wasn't mad at why it had taken me so long to tell her. She agreed to be my muse.

I walked down the streets with her, witnessing her genderlessness. She was an Irish poet from a few hundred years ago, in her Samuel Coleridge coat and glasses. One day she said she was writing a poem about me, and I wanted all of it—to be in the poem and to be the poem and, of course, to read the poem. I liked the real of it, of being next to her in bed, close to her brilliant mind. I was caught up in the idea that together we could go down in history, or maybe go down on each other in herstory. She embodied the idea of my most righteous soul mate, like Gertrude Stein and Alice B. Toklas. John and Yoko. Star-crossed and undeniable.

We took care of each other. *Eileen loves me the way a parent might love a child,* I thought, and it made me think of Ellen, who was still very much alive and fighting. The fact that Ellen's and Eileen's names were so similar annoyed me—never mind the fact that my mom's name is Elaine. This Eileen-Ellen-Elaine holy trinity always dangled as the setup for a real joke where I text the wrong person: *I can't stop thinking about your pussy.*

Eileen wanted to hear everything I was thinking, and then the next thing, and the next thing. Ellen had once said to me that I always get everything I want. And here I was, not just dating a woman, but being loved by the fiercest dyke mind in the universe.

"This is so weird," I said to her one night. "To be in love with someone who loves my mind."

"Is it because I'm a woman?" she asked. "Is that why it's different?"

"I don't know," I said. "All I know is that I never talked this much when I was with men. I don't know if it's because they weren't interested in my mind or if it was because I was trying to create a personality I thought they would find attractive."

"It's hard for me to imagine someone not digging all of this," she said, gesturing at me.

That made me cry.

"I think that back when I dated guys I was trying to win," Eileen said.

"I think so, too," I said. And then added, "What does that mean?"

"It means that there is a sense that being a woman is something you can win at."

WHEN I GOT back home someone had flipped on a switch above L.A. Light that had been pale yellow was deep golden and ochre, the bushes along that fence suddenly had those bursting passionflowers, all tangy purple and white and neon green waving tendrils—were they always there? I walked from Silver Lake all the way to La Brea, stopping for a whole broiled chicken from an *a la brasa* stand and an ice-cold Mexican Coke in a bottle, then kept walking and walking, every three minutes texting Eileen pictures of the world and selfies of myself in it.

Eileen wanted to know the content of the hunger behind my eyes. We were inside of the world together, and my work receded, because she was right there next to my brain—at the stove, when I drove, in the shower. My need for her drooling out of the side of my mouth, waking me at two A.M. to search my drawer for a pen to write what it felt like. Our ideas about the world made themselves alive into shapes to be revealed to each other. There was this new place that was Eileen's heart, a secret address I never knew about. I cried about dumb things like why we didn't meet sooner. I wanted to stroke her hair while she slept, to be cats together. We spoke on the phone every night for hours before bed, texting first thing in the morning. You up? I'm up.

A few weeks later she came to L.A. to visit. I had a small dinner party and invited Cherry Jones, who had since been cast in the show as the poet Leslie Mackinaw, and her new wife over to my house so we could all meet. Eileen liked the fake her. The hair department had cut Cherry's hair like Eileen's and the wardrobe department got clothes like Eileen's. I had written a fictional character who fell in love with a character who was based on a person that the new, somewhat fictional version of me was falling in love with.

A FEW MONTHS into shooting Season Two, the cast and crew gathered around a large TV that had been wheeled onto the set to watch the announcement of the Emmy nominations. I thought back to a time a few years before, when I was a writer on *Six Feet Under.* The morning of the Emmy nominations my stomach was gurgling. I wondered if I was actually going to get nominated. One measly website had one measly mention of my episode "Back to the Garden."

This was very different.

This involved a whole gigantic PR department and some consultants and one wonderful person in particular, Peter Binazeski, who knew all the ins and outs of awards. In fact,

I learned that most TV shows hire entire agencies just to work on awards strategy. Money is spent campaigning, going after every single award you can possibly get, press and features planted across the ecosystem to make the outcome a foregone conclusion. Winning awards doesn't just happen; there must be deep spending and commitment to an industrious series of tactics. Or maybe it did just happen, or maybe it was a little bit of both. The announcements aired. We were nominated for eleven Emmy Awards. The whole team screamed and hugged. A few hours later news vans came and we all went outside to record our up-to-the-minute reactions.

When my friend Robin was married to Mike Myers, she described a chunk of their years together as "the success montage." It came from movies like *Working Girl* or *Tootsie,* the swirling images: the cover of *Rolling Stone,* the red carpet, christening a ship with a bottle of champagne, meeting the Queen. It feels like that when I look back and attempt to name every one of the whoops, the hugging and the chugging.

It felt like everyone was nominated. Jeffrey and Gaby and Bradley Whitford for acting; Marie and Nancy, our costume goddesses; our composer Dustin O'Halloran for *that song* from the title credits; my longtime friend and collaborator Cate Haight, who edited the pilot; and the production designer Cat Smith. The party was a parade just down the road and it was heading toward us.

In the meantime, the things that had happened in the previous year were now being acted out in front of us. We went back to Shatto 39 Lanes to shoot a scene at Lez Bowl, but this time Ali and Syd would fall in love instead of me and Mel.

For the final episode of the season, we brought our Michfest to life at a giant ranch near Ventura. At the end of the episode, Maura and Ali and Maura's mother, Rose, time travel to a hallucinated confrontation in both the woods of the festival and the Tiergarten in Berlin. We spontaneously created a dance between the actors and background artists, all whipped up into a frenzy that felt like street theater, out in a parking lot late at night. Around a big bonfire, they danced an interpretation of a real night when the brownshirts and young proto-Nazis assaulted the queer members of the Institute of Sexology. The Aryan kids smashed glass and carried the books out in stacks as horns played. Books and photos, historical data and medical records of the world's first gender-affirmation surgeries, all thrown onto the fire. People came from everywhere to the Tiergarten to watch this torching of the legacy of Magnus Hirschfeld. The idea of his queer Jewish intellectualism as deviant was one of Hitler's first propagandistic impulses.

For the earlier part of the episode, we shot celebration and queer camp joy. We had hundreds and hundreds and hundreds of extras out there in the woods—every last LGBTQIA person in L.A., including all of Mel's friends and Eileen's people and some BDSM folks. Whenever we shot big crowd scenes, Rhys and Zackary would also pull in their entire community, every artist and postmodern hipster and gender crusader, bikini bottoms and horn-rimmed glasses and leather caps and weird boots. Lots of women were topless. We also gave roles to all of our old friends from the Annoyance Theatre, muses like Becky Thyre, Melanie Hutsell, and Robin Ruzan. All of the writers were there, of course, and Ali Liebegott, who had written the episode, played a festivalgoer who squatted and peed in the background during one of the scenes. The Indigo Girls played, and Sia was there, and I know it's starting to sound like the end of *The Wizard of Oz*—*and you were there, and you were there, Scarecrow.* It was everything and everybody.

The busier things got, the calmer I felt. This intensely creative time of bringing together the past and the present felt unthinkable, a climactic experience artistically and in real life. I could feel it, everything crossing and merging, inevitable, as we danced our heads off for pain and freeddom and love. For past and future.

Bruce had just gotten back from Burning Man and was newly glowing and happy; he brought the woman he was dating. She worked with the artist Alice Boman, whose longing song of spooky melancholy, "Waiting," with the lyrics "Are you coming back?" bookended the whole season. I watched Bruce and his new girlfriend watch Eileen in the audience with her shirt off. At the end of the episode, Ali slides into Leslie's tent. They kiss for the first time, and Leslie unbuttons Ali's shirt as the season comes in for a landing.

WE WENT FROM shooting Nazis and hundreds of naked feminists in a field to the Emmy Awards a few days later. It had been six months since the weirdness of the premiere when I sat with Bruce's family instead of my own, when I had publicly jettisoned my most beloved to outer rows. It was three months after the Golden Globes, when Bruce had escaped with Felix to the mountains to snowboard and Faith and I recommitted to each other.

Things were finally calm and happy. And in a stroke of magic, a stylist named Mariel—one-half of the celebrity team Rob and Mariel—reached out. She was used to dressing Gwen Stefani and Rihanna, but for Goddess knows what reason she got in touch with *this little pisher*, as my mom likes to say. I was invited to a secret address in East Hollywood, where she brushed me past bejeweled stretchy outfits that looked like ice skater wear. "All of that is J.Lo's," Mariel said as we headed toward a private room.

Designers had sent her suits that corresponded with every aspect of the mood board we were working on. In my previous world, I dreamed that I might get clothes for free or at a discount. In Mariel's world, the designers dreamed she might put one of their outfits on someone. *Please put this dress on Kate Moss* or *Get these boots on Rooney Mara, I beg of you.* No one was saying *Please put this suit on Jill Soloway,* but Mariel was using her powers for good and I was grateful. I picked so many suits, and stood on a small platform while three women rushed in like Snow White's birds to measure and pin me.

There we were, all of us looking at me. I had gone on a diet. "Look at you, sample size," Mariel said, and she was right, I was skinny. I was casually telling people that I was about to be the hottest they would ever see me. The word "lewks" hadn't been invented yet, but the idea of a shoe game had and mine was on point.

I had just turned fifty. I didn't know that I didn't want to be femme yet, but I knew I didn't want to dye my hair anymore. There was no way to grow out my roots with long hair, and I was sick of brown-tinted dry shampoo on my collar. After the Emmys it would be time for a rethink.

I asked Mariel to style both me and my moppa, which was probably a boundary violation; anyway she said she didn't have time. I called Isabel, who had been a costume assistant on *Afternoon Delight*, and hired her to pull together some options for Carrie. My mother would take care of herself. *All black*, she says, as in *done*, the original denier of the idea that dressing up femme could be fun.

I really wanted Moppa to be comfortable. At the premiere at the Ace a year before, she'd worn a just-to-the-knee black lace dress that I'd felt was a little too "cousin of the queen of England" for her. I imagined my moppa as more of a sleek artist-in-a-jumpsuit type, maybe someone who had spent time in Paris talking about futurism. I was projecting, I guess, but in a fit of last-minute excitement, I asked if she might be interested in trying on a periwinkle silk jumpsuit that I'd brought but decided not to wear. It might look cute on her. She agreed to try it on.

As I was going up the stairs I ran into Jeffrey and grabbed him. We crammed into Carrie's hotel room, cracking up as she tried to get the jumpsuit on, and fell onto the bed. All three of us laughed from some ancient shtetl place, howls of pre-pogrom village vibes. Jeffrey always used to put me on the floor laughing about his Cousin Yossel, or his grandmother who'd kept carp in the bathtub. Both Carrie and Jeffrey let their sad, self-pitying Yiddishisms inflect their humor, this *Oy vey, why me, why did I tell Jilly I would try on her jumpsuit, five minutes before we were all due to walk the red carpet?* It all added up to us laughing so hard we were almost hyperventilating.

There would be no more last-minute costume changes this time. Or beat changes.

Isabel got some fantastic options, and on the morning of the Emmys, my assistant texted me videos of Carrie trying on clothes. They were all having a lovely morning. I was in a hotel room on the other side of downtown having my own big bride day. Five people looking at my silver sock with arms folded: *Hmm, is that the right amount of sparkle?*

Why were we at separate hotels? We'd continued hurling ourselves as far away from one another as possible, even during a weekend we had planned to spend together. Or maybe it was just me, backing away because they were coming toward me. I would eventually learn to put us all in the same place, like a real family.

But on that day, cars picked us up, and I took a half a Xanax in the back seat while holding tightly onto Isaac's sweaty hand. We gave ourselves calming mantras: *It's just a regular day, it's a regular day in a car and we're going somewhere.* It had been so smart to invite Isaac as my date this time. I had that much figured out. Turn toward the ones you love. How many lifetimes does one need to understand that?

The cars dropped everyone off at the Staples Center. Some of us walked the red carpet in the sweltering heat before we took our seats—it was a hundred degrees in downtown L.A. that day. We had handheld battery-operated fans. The main actors were all there in their finery, as were Trace and Melora and others from our chosen family.

I had prepared for the possibility of going onstage and winning three times. I was nominated for writing and directing, and the show was also nominated. I hated when people pretended to not prepare speeches, getting onstage and saying, *I didn't expect this.* I mean, please. It's all any of us have been dreaming about since we were kids. The golden statues as nerd touchdowns at the homecoming game.

Preparing for the possibility of three wins could be considered a delusion of grandeur. Or should that diagnosis only be an insult reserved for cis white guys? *Is* it delusional to try to suggest to yourself that it is okay to believe you might be magnificent when the world raised you to mostly admire men, to reserve grandiosity or genius only for them?

On my morning walks, I practiced my Emmy speech. Okay fine, all three of them. How could I not get myself ready for that thirty seconds to speak to the world live? I was afraid to imagine the biggest version of the night and afraid not to. My childhood heroes weren't baseball stars—they were James L. Brooks, Norman Lear, Sherwood Schwartz, Jim Burrows. Maybe I was going to stand where they had stood.

I loved that the speeches didn't have to be about me. They were about all of the new trans people in the industry, our crew family, our new world, our Topple Productions methods of creating, and our process, and that made me feel solar powered. The eight-year-old who had wanted to be the first female president refused to pretend she didn't want the airtime. She wanted to change the world, and so did I.

The night of the Emmys, I saw my face on the big screen behind the stage, along with four men. And then they called my name; I won for directing the pilot. I laughed and high-fived Isaac. When I got onstage I looked out at Moppa in the audience and talked about how, in the majority of states in this country, it would be perfectly legal for a landlord to sit across from her and say, *Sorry, no, we don't rent to trans people.* Being up there felt terrifying and just right. I know how to do this, I told myself, how to be present and feel it.

I went offstage and waited.

Took a deep breath.

Jeffrey's category was next. Bradley Whitford and I watched from backstage as Jeffrey won. He came back with his award and we all flew into the air at each other.

We walked under scaffolding to a hall and someone took the Emmy out of my hands and I went to a table to get a different one, this one with an assigned serial number, which they wrote in a ledger. Then someone handed me McDonald's fries, which was exactly what I wanted in that moment, and a vodka drink, which I sipped, and it kind of helped the throbbing and vibrating in my head. We floated into something like a shopping mall, but instead of stores it was filled with media outlets. You walk with your statues and your PR people decide to whom you should talk and who wants to talk to you. Each station has couches and there's a relaxed, high-end browsing feel, women with perfect eyebrows and men in creamy matte talking to you ebulliently, as if we're all old friends. Flowers and carpets and warm interviewers welcome you again and again into the moment.

After that I was escorted into a press room, where hundreds of reporters and more photographers were sitting in rows on risers. Jeffrey and I talked about trans politics. We took pictures together. People yelled at me to kiss the statue. I did.

Then we went back to our seats to see if we'd win for best show, but *Veep* did. It all ended and we gathered and went to the Governors Ball next door. People were looking for secret places to smoke pot and by the time we got in, there was an enormous purple central revolving stage with Andrea Bocelli atop. In that cavernous room full of people, we were some of the few holding the gold, and every person we passed gave us glowing eye contact: *you did it*.

An official man came over to me and asked if I could come to a roped-off area to get my statue engraved. I took Isaac. We went to a special counter and people with white gloves took the Emmy from me. Isaac and I watched as a machine etched my name into the black band at the base of the statue. A photographer snapped photos of me gazing at Isaac while he looked at the engraving. The guys handed me the statue and we headed back toward our family and the rest of the ball.

I ran into someone who wanted to introduce me to Mel Brooks. Mel told me that he and Carl Reiner had watched *Transparent* together with TV trays on their laps in Carl's living room. I hugged him and he held me. I think he knew how much I needed him. He asked where we were going later and then promised to come by the Amazon party to see us. I wanted to marry him right there.

We tromped from event to event, making ourselves into a crumbled comedy pyramid on the floor as the flashbulbs popped at one of the parties. We kept going until that feeling crept in when you wonder why you are still out. We were all in the right place at the right time and we could feel it.

At the end of the night, people came up to congratulate me as I sat in a booth with Mel Brooks. I had sleepy eyes and he wrapped his arms around me like a papa bear. He seemed like he was proud.

THERE WERE SO many moments like this one, all of them rushing by in the success montage, so so fast. Going to the White House to be honored as part of a "Champions of Change" event—my moppa in classy gray pants and a blouse and a scarf, me taking pictures of her in front of the flags at the entrance. Eileen was there in her Kennedy coat and posed for a picture next to the oil painting of President Kennedy. All of the trans women on *Transparent* dressed up in First Lady America Queer Edition finery; as a delegation we filled the First Lady's salon. I kept telling myself, *Feel this feel this feel this.*

Did I mention the Peabody Awards or being onstage at a premiere to introduce Norman Lear, and then Norman Lear coming to the writers' room and telling us about when he was a fighter pilot? Did Darren Aronofsky really compare me to Philip Roth? Going to London for the European release? Awards made of Lucite and so many hotel rooms and awkward glam sessions? The night with David E. Kelley and Shonda Rhimes or the AFI event where I talked to Meryl Streep? Katy Perry had the whole cast over for dinner. She wanted to meet the cast of *Transparent* because she was a fan. Caitlyn Jenner was there, too. That night, Judith Light shared with us her favorite Kierkegaard quote: "Life can only be understood backward; but it must be lived forward."

We all nodded, secretly aware that to act like we knew what she meant would be to miss the point of the quote.

10   WE'RE NOT ALLOWED TO WANT

MAZON WANTED ME TO GO TO GERMANY TO DO PRESS IN EARLY December, so Eileen and I planned a trip to Paris over Thanksgiving. When I told my mom that I wouldn't be spending the holiday with my kids, she suggested I cancel the part with Eileen and just do the press. "Your kids will never forgive you," she said. Felix went to Hawaii with Bruce and was fine. Isaac was at first angry that he had to go to a friend's grandmother's house in Philly, then found he loved it so much he never wanted to spend his holidays anywhere else.

The plane ride to Paris was amazing. We felt so grateful to have found ourselves in this moment. There were only three people in the quiet, first-class cabin, which looked like the Jetsons' living room. It was just us and a wealthy woman from Dallas who was going to Christmas fairs across Europe even though she swore she didn't have even one inch of space on her shelves. There were two flight attendants wholly dedicated to the three of us. They offered us light blue pajamas, and we took turns going into the bathroom to put them on, then emerged and handed the attendants our clothes on hangers. We sat in our seats like good students, our trays up and laps flat, legs straight out, waiting for the time when we would be allowed to recline more.

After we were in the pajamas, the captain came out to tell us both how happy he was to have us on the flight. Then the co-captain came over to tell us how happy *he* was to have us on the flight. The attendants served us steak and cream of asparagus soup. I got a Bloody Mary, and they made beds for us in our seats. We each took half an Ambien and fell asleep. It seemed we were in Paris in an instant. When we awoke, we hazily dashed to the airplane bathroom to change out of our pajamas and back into our street clothes while the flight attendants made our beds back into chairs.

We were whisked off the plane and through customs without so much as a bag being opened, then took a limo ride into the city and checked into the Hotel de Pavillon des Reines. The courtyard twinkled with pale blue and white lights, and there was this incredible scent in the lobby. Every time I walked through during that entire week, I would think: *How I can take a picture of this soft smoldering wood smell?*

We took naps and then went out for a walk. The Vietnamese place that Yelp had suggested was closed when we got there, so we ended up in a weird Chinese dive with linoleum floors and menus with heavy red cloth and faded gold tassels. Over noodles, we talked about our childhoods. Eileen told me the story of the day she and her siblings watched her father push a bureau out of the third-floor window of their childhood house, and how he went crashing down along with it. She talked about how he tried to recover over the next few months but never really got back to normal, and how he died while she was in the room with him, just a little girl doing her homework trying not to see what she was seeing.

There were no majorly traumatic moments in my childhood—not at our house, anyway. No explosions, no falls, but I do remember a little boy I didn't know, a few houses down, who killed his brother by accident with his father's gun. My parents were wrecked, and I responded in the way of six-year-olds, moving on quickly. As I tried to stack up the experiences for Eileen of how it felt to be five-ish to eleven-ish, I found it all incredibly murky.

I remembered that we had dinner every night in a reliable routine. My mom adhered to advice from an article suggesting that busy and overwhelmed women should serve the same meals on a weekly rotation—so each Monday was pork chops with Campbell's mushroom soup and Minute Rice. Tuesdays were spaghetti straight from the box, covered in Ragu from the jar and browned ground beef with the grease poured off. There was no spice, nary a grain of salt, not a flake of oregano. I'm not complaining. I know that I was lucky to have regular meals, and that everyone feels like their childhood wasn't quite right. Each of us holds on to a hidden map of all of the ways we didn't get nurtured.

There were years when we were happy, when things felt normal. Then my dad went back to medical school to be a psychiatrist and started analysis. When I think back on it, he might have sought pharmaceutical help, maybe amphetamines so he could stay up all night to study. My mom got a job at Habitat, the organization that ran South Commons, and one day hauled her red IBM Selectric typewriter home from work and into the downstairs den. It was her first home office, and my dad could hear the tapping on the typewriter all the way in his bedroom, so he came downstairs bellowing to get that fucking typewriter out of the house. On another night when we had kids over for a slumber party, he burst in, raging in front of our friends because our laughing was too loud. Now other people could see.

"Did Dad rage three or four times, or a hundred?" I asked my sister, and then my mom. Collectively, we were never able to make a true accounting. "It's just that we were always on eggshells and afraid to wake him," my mom said.

I remembered that when I was eight or nine I started standing up for my mom.

"You are not allowed to talk to her like that," I would say, putting my body between the two of them.

"OH, YOU STAY OUT OF IT!" he would scream. Faith was always over there, playing piano, flying under the radar.

Sometimes I heard people say, "And then I went home for Passover and we had the *best* time!" or "It just feels *so* good to walk into my house at the end of the day!" I used to think, *Who are these people for whom home is respite?* I was well into being an adult when I realized that some homes are places where people create joy by taking turns being really nice to each other. *I cooked your favorite thing! No*, you *relax; I'll go get us some water. I was at the bookstore and I saw this and thought of you, so I bought it.* Do some people live in these small tribes where they actually actively want to nourish and replenish one another's wells?

Everything in my childhood home felt like a competition.

Maybe this was why it had felt so natural for me all those years to set up systems with Bruce, systems so stringent that we never checked in, and instead accrued righteous accounts of our own pain.

FAITH HAS REMINDED me that there were lots of sweet things, too. Every Sunday night, we would go to the same restaurant, the Hickory Pit in Bridgeport, where we had a family ritual. We would open our menus, and Faith would say, "How much can I spend, Dad?" Our family had enough money; there was no reason for Faith to worry about the price of what she ordered. But Faith and Dad were making a subtle joke about us performing a skit as a family who could order only the cheapest thing. And even though it was a performance, Faith would always end up ordering the cheapest dish, and then she would have to eat it, whether it was what she wanted or not. No one was really allowed to want anything.

Maybe the ritualized dinners my mom prepared were her way of putting a container around the lack of control she felt in a marriage that was falling apart from the inside. What were the things she unconsciously did to protect all of us from this hidden chaos? Her husband, who was really a woman, was going to therapy five days a week, being told that cross-dressing was a fetish. My trans parent, told by an expert that their self would have to be stopped, cut off, discontinued if they wanted to have a successful family life.

———

MY PARENTS HAD met when they were in college, and they fell madly in love. Harry was a real catch—Jewish, pre-med, funny, so tall and so British. He was sophisticated and foreign and not at all like the other West Side Chicago boys. There was only one problem: he was my mom's friend Lynda's boyfriend. I used to ask my mom to tell me the story over and over again, about the time she won Daddy from that girl. When she had hung out with Lynda and my dad, my dad would give my mom special looks. One day he called her. *Can we talk alone?* She says she thought he was going to ask her advice about an engagement ring. Instead, he had said: "I don't love Lynda. I love you."

That was the line I loved the most. *Tell me again, Mommy.*

They started sneaking around and meeting in places where no one could find them. When my mom's mom, Minnie, found out, she'd insisted they break up. If word got out that my mom had stolen my dad from Lynda, the whole neighborhood would turn on them. One day, they finally came clean. Lynda was crushed; my dad proposed to my mom to make it all good as quickly as possible.

Now I see a shadowy, poetic shape within my mom and dad's initial connection: a competition between two women, and an unspoken agreement to keep secrets.

In their wedding picture, my mom is wearing a borrowed cream lace dress and cat's-eye glasses. There must have been a glare on her lenses in the original photo because when you look closely at the album you can see that her eyes were drawn in with a shaky black pen. Rudimentary early Photoshop attempts.

My dad finished med school, and then joined the army,

as all dads did back then. They spent a few years doing military life on an army base in Fort Devens, Massachusetts. In more photos from this time, my dad is always in a white T-shirt, black glasses, dark buzz cut. All of my mom's friends back home were getting pregnant, but for a long time my mom couldn't. And then, finally, she did, with my sister, Faith.

Faith's baby pictures show her big eyebrows and disdain for the poufy outfits they put her in. In the fancy department-store portrait-studio photos, she looks like she was plopped down accidentally into a dress. A year or so after she was born, they left the army base and moved back to Chicago. In 1965 they had me, a little girl who seemed more like a girl and loved dollies.

My parents first tried to raise us in the suburbs of Chicago, in a development called The Willows. My mom told me that after spending afternoons at the sandbox with the other moms, she would come home and cry alone. She didn't fit in. She felt like she was living someone else's life. The other moms took diet pills and talked about vacuum cleaners. She wanted out.

After she read an article in the *Chicago Sun-Times* glorifying the social experiment New Town of South Commons, she monologized at my dad for months, saying that she could feel it in her bones that we had to move there.

It turned out to be everything the developers promised, the moms sitting on their porches, drinking their white wine or Tabs while they watched the children play. Elaine put out her weekly newsletter. Today she would have syndicated her column, turned it into a career. But women weren't doing that then; there was no path, so she did what so many of us did with our lives—wasted her creative energy hoping to get men to like or love her. While my dad was back in med school reinventing himself from anesthesiologist to psychiatrist, and attempting to understand the mystery of transness in analysis, my mom was having a lot of affairs.

There was one day in South Commons when Faith and I were playing with the kids next door, hurling dirt clumps at passing cars. The clumps were filled with hard things that looked like onions, mud balls with nuts inside them. Soon, one of the neighborhood moms approached us, and she was furious. We had unearthed an entire bed of the tulip bulbs she'd planted.

A few decades later my mom confessed over Chardonnay that the tulip day was the day she'd started an affair with a jazz musician. Maybe when that other mom was yelling, my mom heard, "Look what you did. You went out and let some man have sex with you, and while you did that, your kids destroyed my garden. *You* destroyed my garden, all future beauty."

In the early seventies, there was no way my dad could have come out, even to herself. The only trans women anyone ever heard about were spectacles, tragic figures on *The Phil Donahue Show.* My parents stayed together. Maybe they were afraid of what loneliness would feel like, how hard it is to carry yourself through the world alone, without that permanent other promising you that they will help. Instead of divorcing, our parents left Faith and me with a decent set of memories around whatever childhood is supposed to be.

There were beautiful, raucous times. We did community theater. On the weekends we tromped as a family to rehearsals at the nearby Trinity Church, a gigantic Catholic castle on the corner that looked like it was made of dripped sand and Jerusalem stone. Adults and kids came together to put on different plays each year—Gilbert and Sullivan or Rodgers and Hammerstein musicals like *Pirates of Penzance* and *Carousel*. My mom produced these shows, always powerful and effective, mimeographing the programs. My dad usually played the lead, presenting male, but occasionally in full makeup as the Mikado, belting out songs in a warm tenor. Faith and I were always in the chorus, in homemade costumes. Opening nights and cast parties gave birth to scenes of gangs of my parents' friends who all looked like characters in those old Woody Allen movies, singing around the piano long into the night. We were protected from our parents' secrets, playing hard day and night in the quadrangle, the adults singing and sleeping together and downing bourbons, for years. Group gatherings were things we did until people got the chance to go to their corners, alone—an affair with a stranger, cross-dressing in private, Faith on the piano.

And where was I? Is this true, that I was already defined as that kid who got close to winning but instead chose to go back, saying forget it, over and over and over again? Sounds right. Fuck bike riding or swimming, sports or hobbies. I think I leaned on a cushion and watched my mom write.

AFTER DINNER AT the Chinese restaurant, Eileen and I went back to the hotel and I changed into my nightgown, which Eileen called my *shmata*. Bruce used to call this nightgown "flagrant," like how dare I flagrantly walk around the house so not-sexy, so not aware of how much I was *not*, even in the privacy of our own home, making myself into something intended to turn him on.

Eileen and I lay in bed together and did a speakerphone reading of our astrological transits with an astrologer from New York. I found out I was in a leadership cycle that would go until 2031. Ugh. That sounded exhausting.

Then we decided to watch some porn. Neither of us was much into feminist or queer porn. We decided to check out the stankiest, rankest, cis-hetero versions—only for research, of course. We found a genre called Trick Your Girlfriend. You start with a regular, somewhat Balkan-appearing young boy, whispering on the phone with his friend, inviting him over. He hangs up, walks over to his girlfriend, and kisses her. He lightly suggests BDSM and ties her arms to the headboard and blindfolds her. She consents to their private, albeit tied-up sex, but soon enough the buddy appears (that was fast; he must live in the apartment next door) and (*shhhhh!!!*) then the buddy fucks the blindfolded girlfriend (WHAT!?) while the original guy watches, smirking (but strangely enough, not jerking off). That unspoken dialogue: *hey, come over, let's both get our dicks out. Okay! I'm on my way!*

I had always found this fascinating, this genre of men wanting to have sex in the same room as each other, but using a woman as the degraded half of the Divided Feminine in order not to name their desires for each other's gaze or body.

"Your purpose is to heal the Divided Feminine," I remembered Joan Scheckel saying to me, and then I thought about how Jacques Lacan characterized women as temporary phalluses. He saw how an admired, beautiful woman could be a projected object, a temporary external attachment. *I date this younger, hotter woman and therefore I am a better version of myself when she stands next to me.*

I wish Lacan had investigated the way a man's most vulnerable version of himself gets projected onto a woman he disrespects. The slut, the sex worker, the stripper, the woman who drinks too much to be able to do her assigned job as a reliable consenter. The degraded woman as an adjunct vagina, not a phallus. This thing that gets what it deserves, a proxy for men's own dreams of what it would mean to move from non-consent into consent, widening desire as the bridge.

The other video we watched involved a girl who was locked out of her apartment. She knocked on this guy's apartment door. He let her in and was going to call the locksmith to help her out. But wait, he'll call the locksmith in just one second. In the meantime, maybe she should take off her clothes. Once she got her clothes off, ostensibly so that the locksmith would be called, the one guy told his buddy to come in from the other room. Then he watched his buddy fuck her. She was only doing it so the other guy would call the locksmith; at one point, the buddy came all over her face. Then the first guy told the truth—there was never any locksmith—and made her leave and go out to the hallway holding her clothes. Eileen made the *wah wah wah* game show game-over sound. That night we had great sex. Even bad porn works that way.

The next day we walked the rainy streets of Paris. It was Thanksgiving. We went to the place that supposedly had the best croissants in the world, and they were good, maybe even that good. We held hands and when we came to the hitching posts at the edges of the alleys our hands didn't know if they should rise in a little wave or let go and quickly reclamp. The Bataclan attacks had happened a few days before and the world seemed like it was going to end. We had to do something. We were still so mad about the porn. How could you be a woman and watch those videos and still want to be a woman? How could you see all of the prompts on the site asking you to choose between *Brit milf spunked in mouth after doggystyled* and *Creampie coed wants your cum in her pussy* and still be thrilled to walk around in the world female? And why did it work to turn us on?

The contradictions were so intense that we decided there was only one solution: we had to write a manifesto that would bring about a feminist revolution, that would transform our current epoch into a Utopian age, and, in particular, that would do all this by making it illegal for men to make porn.

We went back to the hotel room and ordered some tea. I typed as Eileen dictated. Every ten minutes we would switch places. We laughed because it was so serious, this notion that all we needed to do was write the one thing that no one had said yet. This is one of the reasons Eileen and I loved each other. We both want to go down in history. She was so much closer to going down in history than I was but still. In that moment we both believed fully that our love could unite and catalyze our minds into one earth-shattering voice. All we had to do was get it down.

THE THANKSGIVING PARIS MANIFESTO

We shouldn't be starting with porn but we must.

We support the idea of a porn industry and the idea of people making a living photographing and sharing images of sex, but we don't support an industry that exclusively distributes portrayals of almost exclusively male pleasure and climax.

Similarly, we support the idea of government and the right of people to both expect and to deliver society, safety, and services to other people, but we don't support any government that exclusively supplies systems created almost exclusively of male ideology and triumph.

Thus, to begin a revolution, we are demanding a climate of reparation:

Porn made by men is hereby outlawed for one hundred years (one full century).

In all other arts and representations, i.e.: film, television, books, poetry, songwriting, and architecture, fifty years (one half-century) will be adequate for the ban.

These measures, while extreme, are the only method through which we can experience what authentic female representation would truly look like. We don't see this as a punishment, but rather an offering of an opportunity for all people, especially men, to operate within a female-constructed reality.

War is a cultural invention dreamed up by men; it is a product of their governing and government. We intend to permanently end war.

Implicit herein is an indictment of racism. In the U.S. and globally, a police force enacts war culture and perpetuates and endorses violence and terror on the local level, person to person. The implementation of this cultural product employs the narrative that positions lighter-skinned peoples above darker-skinned peoples. Our intention is to disrupt this forever.

We thereby and hereby demand an immediate end to male government. Male-constructed governing must cease for one hundred years (one century).

All primary positions of power (including but not limited to presidents and queens, prime ministers, cabinet ministers and their ombudsmen, kings, comptrollers, their representatives and congresspeople, alderpeople, senators, lords, and mayors) must be held by female-identified or vagina-bodied people. In addition, the congresses and governing bodies supervised by and working in concert with said positions of power must be held by female-identified or vagina-bodied people.

Regarding the global economy, we have no specific recommendations, but feel that the preceding actions and demands will have vast repercussions. Have no fear: just as industrialization and factories marked the end of an agrarian sense of time, the invention of the computer and the Internet allow for a newly Utopian way of life: a fresh definition of work and who needs to do it.

In our understanding the cause of the current problem is that very few men are handing down edicts to the mass of men. Many men feel badgered, repressed, wounded, unrewarded, and swollen with hurt by this state of things. We want to invite men to enthusiastically join us in the toppling of this artificial masculinist hierarchy. We know the current cultural, sociological, political, and spiritual expectations and definitions of maleness have robbed you of your manhood, of your strongest heart. We know you also look at killing and feel: I will not. What we will do:

1. Bury our guns. We ask you to dig mass graves for pistols, rifles, AK-47s, hand grenades, bombs, toy guns, squirt guns, or whatever you can put your hand on that hurts. We encourage you to identify unused real estate in your area or neighborhood and please use it to this end.
2. God = Kindness.
3. With the invention of computers, the world is now wired for Armageddon. The Middle East has always represented the beginning and the end of the world. As a real and symbolic measure, we invite all people (who feel as we do) to go to Jerusalem. Let us stand there, at the borders forever, holding hands to protect that space. We declare a new inevitable of peace in which the Female Face of God will show.
4. Our document is weaponless. Our bravest offering is our time and our very lives. Stand with us now.

We finished the manifesto and read it aloud a couple of times. *This is it,* we thought. *We will change the world. The world sucked, but now it is better.*

I emailed my assistant Courtney back in L.A. at the office and asked her to buy the domain name Topplethe patriarchy.com. I told her that a very important document was coming, and to please let me know EXACTLY when the website was ready. Then and only then would I email this *very important document.* And if for some reason Eileen and I should die in a terrorist attack, come to Paris and get my computer and get the manifesto and put it up on the website.

That might be hard, I thought. Okay, to be safe, I sent Courtney the manifesto the next day, punching the keys hard on my laptop.

This. Is. It.

We did it.

As Eileen and I walked to the train station, we checked Twitter. Are people retweeting it yet? No, not yet. But we knew they would. Maybe the revolution would have started by the time we got to Germany.

WE WAITED FOR our train at the Gare du Nord. I loved the way the bells sounded in the Paris train station. Three spooky notes. The breathy announcements of track numbers in a woman's apologetic hushed voice.

The Night Train from Paris to Berlin sounded like the title of a short story. We boarded and settled in. Across from me, Eileen pulled out a book, gobbling up Herman Melville's *Pierre*. Reading it was making her want to read even more, she said, it was making her want to read Emily Dickinson. She had no fear of how busy and complex her brain could possibly get; she wanted it all. She fed herself like she was both the mom and her very own genius little boy.

We checked into our hotel room in Berlin. I would do press in the morning to promote Season Two. I'd been trying to avoid the reviews because I was nervous about how the Magnus Hirschfeld stuff would be received. I was getting into the bath when I saw the first review. It was *Time* magazine. The reviewer hated the season.

I'd fucked up.

It was so shocking to see myself being seen by such a wide lens. I dropped into that feeling: *Jill, you got it all wrong again.* Worse than a shame spiral, a big self-hatred bath. It's always waiting for me. Then the next reviews came out and they were fine. Great, even. This fucking ride. The gut wrench of the first bad review. It was impossible to recover. I wanted so badly to be like those people who don't read press. How do they do it?

The next day I was scheduled to speak to some Amazon executives. They sent over a delightful German gentleman to do my glam. Under bright lights, he came at me with liquid liner, and I found myself backing away from him. He kept coming at me and I kept backing away.

Finally, when I was against the wall, I burst out, "Stop it!"

"Am I doing somezing wrong?" he asked.

Here I was, preparing to go downstairs to speak about business, about creativity and television, and a man had been sent to my room to draw a new face on top of my actual face. Why was I expected to be a pretty lady? Why did I need an entirely different face in order to speak?

The glam man retreated. And in that moment I thought, *What if I never ever wore makeup again?*

I did the event, and then that night, in bed, Eileen and I held each other.

"Are you okay?" she asked.

"Yeah," I said. "So hey, would you still love me if . . ."

"If what?" she asked.

"If I was butch?"

"You are butch," she teased.

"No, I mean I want to get rid of this, all this curly hair, these clothes, no more makeup. I mean, what if I was this other thing?"

"Ya know, I've dated people before," she said, "who weren't sure if they wanted to be with me or *be* me. This woman Camille, after we broke up, she went totally butch. And then she transitioned. You don't want to transition, do you?" she asked.

"Of course not," I said.

We fell asleep, holding on to each other.

11   YOU GOT WHAT YOU WANTED

WHEN I CAME HOME FROM PARIS, I CALLED ISAAC TO FIND OUT WHO cut his hair at Vinny's, the hipster spot on Virgil in East Hollywood. He told me the guy's name was Angel, but that I could go only if I promised not to say one word about being his mom.

I loved going to the barber. They handed me a beer when I walked in, and Angel didn't talk during the cut at all. All the customers seemed to be in a dull, floating meditation, a few of them with eyes closed as their barber coated the back of their neck in hot foam. No one said, "Cute shoes!" or asked, "So are you going out tonight?"

I saw my new self in the mirror.

I left the barbershop and looked one more time in my car's sun visor mirror. Took a few photos. Sent one to Eileen. Then one to my mom. Now I looked more like her.

That afternoon as I was heading out with Felix, I suddenly realized that "getting ready" no longer existed, not even the barest minimum. I was wearing denim shorts and a T-shirt. With my short hair, I was now already ready, all the time. I was just a head, a face. No side sheath of bangs or hair to hide behind. Felix and I walked to a friend's house down the street, and he bounded off to play in the yard. The adults congregated in mostly gendered huddles, and I found myself in the kitchen with the dads, debating hard about some political idea. I slowly realized that in the past, when I was straight and femme, I would have never hung out with the dads for that long. I wouldn't have inserted myself into their circle and held forth. I wouldn't have wanted them, or their wives, to think I was flirting.

As the weeks passed I found that I was much more comfortable in the world. I felt free to express myself more clearly, newly interested in having real conversations. In being present. How could such a distinct mind and mood change come with a haircut?

Over the next few months, I started to wonder how it would feel if I could interact with people without them projecting identities on me: dykey woman, cute girl, loud lady, lousy mom, cool man, short mannish human. I began to experiment in my mind with the idea of identifying as nonbinary. What if I wasn't female but I also wasn't male? What if I wasn't cis but also wasn't trans? What if I was everything and nothing at the same time? What would we call that?

I thought of what Julia Serano calls oppositional sexism, which, she says, is

> the assumption is that masculinity is strong while femininity is weak, that masculinity is tough while femininity is fragile, that masculinity is rational while femininity is irrational, that masculinity is serious while femininity is frivolous, that masculinity is functional while femininity is ornamental, that masculinity is natural while femininity

is artificial, and that masculinity is sincere while feminin-
ity is manipulative.

Also known as the air. Under patriarchy. How women, girls, and femmes are fighting this all of the time, all day, every day.

As we find our voices, we first have to describe the conditions of our confinement. The previous decades now seemed lit by a hot spotlight insisting that what I look like matters more than who I am, and power belongs entirely to men, and the only power I get is that which men offer me in exchange for being impressed with me. In the current reality, I can get money from men who are impressed with my storytelling, or I can build a family with men who are impressed with my body and sex and mothering talents. I thrive or fail based on my ability to hold their projections about femininity, which are often corrupted or degraded or disrupted by their feelings about their own femininity. I started to wonder what it would feel like if I could peel back these layers of projection. I thought about how I am as a parent, how I am seen and how I see myself.

I'm the best father in the world. I'm far better as a father than I am as a mother. Imagine a dad like this: Every day at six P.M. I get home from my really high-powered job where I make plenty of money for everybody. I have taken care of dinner by checking in with the sitter on the phone at around three and saying, "Yes, turkey meatballs will be perfect! Maybe we should have some broccoli just to be safe?" Then when I get home dinner is on the table, and I thank the sitter and dismiss her, as I sit with my children and hold space for questions about their day. After dinner, I spend time with them and then put them to bed.

If you imagined a man doing the things I just described, you would think of him as an exceptionally emotionally connected and gentle man. A veritable master of the universe, doing everything at home and at work.

But look at me as a mother: I didn't pick my kids up after school. I didn't actually cook the dinner. We didn't do crafts, sports, or homework together. I wasn't a school volunteer. I wasn't warm and yummy and soft and cozy. I didn't rock them in my arms. I didn't make breakfast. I got no housework done. I didn't get to the gym. And I didn't do that thing they tell wives to do: I didn't have sex whether or not I wanted to; I didn't keep the marriage going.

If I were a man I'd be in the top 1 percent of all fathers. As a mother, I was a complete and total failure.

DURING THE PANEL discussion when I'd first met Eileen, I shared with the audience a question that I'd been considering ever since my dad came out: "If the secret was the boundary, and then the secret is gone, where are our new boundaries?"

At first, *Transparent* became a boundary from the reality of my real family. A place to hold it all out there so I could decide how much of it to let in. My directing technique became another way of defining boundaries. Now I realized that femininity had been a false boundary between myself and my ability to feel at home in the world, embodied. As each aspect of external femme performance dropped away, I reclaimed another piece of my wholeness.

EILEEN CAME TO VISIT. As soon as she saw me, she tousled my hair.

"You look just right, huh?" she told me.

"Like a boy," I said.

"Yup, so cute."

But I'm probably not your type anymore, right? I thought.

Later that day she came to the set with me. We were shooting Ali breaking up with Leslie. In the episode, Leslie is staying at Ali's house, laid up with a broken ankle. She wants Ali to stay home and take care of her, but Ali wants to do some detective work at the mall, to look for clues about the accidental death of Rita, Josh's ex. But because people often lie rather than go through the difficulty of generating authentic boundaries, Ali doesn't want to tell Leslie where she's going. She wants to be alone in the space inside of her lie. Intimacy has become codependence and she wants out. Leslie wants a big kiss. Ali gives her a perfunctory peck. Unfulfilled needs everywhere.

Eileen was sitting in a director's chair with headphones on watching when we both realized that she was watching a fictionalized version of what hadn't yet happened between us.

I stepped over to the set to give Gaby a new playable action: "Maybe try 'escape' instead of 'leave.' Maybe perfunctory, less annoyed, you want to get out fast. You're faking everything at this point."

We shot the scene again, and Eileen watched Gaby play

the moment with more intensity. Gaby got it. Leslie got it. Eileen got it.

This is what is dumb about a television show that sometimes follows your real life. You think things you're not quite ready to say, and then the words come out in your characters' voices and actions. Suddenly everyone can hear them. Everything gets jumbled. Especially when people come to visit the set.

Eileen and I pantomimed through the next few days, trying to pretend we hadn't just witnessed that scene. We talked about what it would be like to be two dudes in love. Could we do that? Of course we could. We weren't with each other for the clothes.

But Eileen went back to New York and as the weeks passed, we stopped showing up for each other: talking just a little less on the phone, *Actually, I can't talk now, I'll try you tonight*, then a text: *I'm sorry I'm so tired, let's just try tomorrow.*

Last call before bed and first thing in the morning became one or two days in between.

"I always thought you might be a jumper," Eileen said.

"Don't say that," I said.

It was time to break up, but I was so scared to be without her in the world. Her brain was crack for me. I had gone from being a baby dyke to a wannabe soft stud. Is it my queerness that said move on? My poly-heartedness? That anxiety snowball racing down the mountain at my back that I inherited from my mom? The one that told me to keep moving, keep moving?

"Can we stay friends?" I asked.

"We'll be friends again soon," she said. And I believed her.

———

I THREW MYSELF back into work and taking care of my family. Felix's birthday was coming up, so I asked him where he wanted to have his party.

"I want to go back to Travel Town and do a train birthday like last year. Do it exactly like that again."

"I think we should try something new," I suggested. "There's a brand-new gym in Frogtown! Let's do it there!"

I googled and showed him the bright, loft-like interior of the new gym. "Fine," he said, "the gym in Frogtown, but there has to be a magician. There was an animal magician who performed at summer camp; I want him."

I googled "animal magician" faster than you can say "animal magician" and I had a picture of him on the screen, surrounded by his animals.

"THAT'S HIM!" Felix said, thrilled.

"GREAT!" I said, snapping the computer closed. New gym in Frogtown, animal magician, DONE. Box checked, emails sent, anxiety of kid's birthday party planning SOLVED, now off to start our day.

A few days later I got an email back from the new gym in Frogtown that said construction wouldn't be finished until a few months after Felix's birthday. *But* they were still doing birthday parties in their previous location, which was connected to Felix's old preschool. Also, the animal magician no longer did birthday parties. But he highly recommended his friend Simon. He's the *best*, the animal magician's email to me insisted.

When the big day finally arrived, Felix had doubts from

the moment he woke up: "I don't want to go to my party today," he said.

Jesus Christ, it's already starting, I thought.

Instead, I said, "Don't worry, sweetie, everyone's anxious before big events."

It was my week with Felix, and Bruce had texted that he was in Pasadena and couldn't help set up the party, so I would have to handle the logistics by myself.

Felix and I drove to the gym. We got out of the car and went inside. The whole place looked sad, and the smell of disinfectant hung heavy in the air. The smell penetrated my forehead and clung to my face. It was inescapable.

Felix turned around and walked back to the parking lot and declared that no, he would not be attending this party. He saw through me: I'd hastily arranged a gym he didn't want and hired an animal magician who, it turned out, had no animals. The other moms were kind as they passed me in the parking lot, pacing like a defense attorney.

All of the kids were in the gym doing their pre-party gym activities when Bruce finally showed up. Oh thank God, maybe he could save us. But not so fast: Felix wouldn't let Bruce talk to him. I calmly sat next to him, pretending like it really didn't matter if we ever went in. I watched Bruce near the main doors. He was on his phone. Probably texting his new girlfriend. I took a picture of him texting madly, texted it to him.

—Why did you do that? he texted back.
—I did that instead of telling you to get off your
   phone.
—I know.

The gym portion of the birthday party was halfway over by the time I finally convinced Felix to go inside. Some combo of threats and shame and probably a bribe finally got him out onto the floor to do some somersaults into foam ball pits with the other kids.

I went to the buffet we'd made on crappy folding tables and swigged some wine. There was pizza for the kids, and I'd rescued a tray of artisanal sandwiches and a fruit platter from an office party the day before. I had asked my assistant to drop off some support Brie. Now I stared at the sad supermarket Brie with the plastic wrap indentations in it and the gross crackers she had plopped onto paper plates with two plastic forks.

It was ugly.

I wanted to throw it all away.

The somersaulting part was over and then the pizza part was over and it was time for the non-animal magician to perform. He was wearing a shiny mint green vest and had dyed brown hair and a patchy porny mustache. He was mean to the children and sexist, calling the girls pretty princesses and making jokes about how the boys needed to start wining and dining them. When he wasn't promoting heteronormativity, he was trying to get the kids to be quiet. There was so much hushing and so much preamble and very little magic. All of the kids seemed to know the size of the mistakes I had made.

A mom told me to have another glass of wine. She shared a tale about a birthday party where Spider-Man came and his suit was so thin you could see his huge bulge of junk. The children were scared. That sounded awful. But this felt worse.

Someone from the gym went to grab some garbage bags to put the presents in, but the garbage bags had that horrible scented odor and created a bad smell storm with the stench of disinfectant from the floors.

I was so mad that because I am a woman it had fallen into my lap to organize the party, and also to do everything else that created our children's lives: to buy clothes and make summer plans and babysitter arrangements and school deliverables and sports sign-ups and health forms. I wanted Bruce to figure out the party while I skulked off and checked my texts. I wanted his parents to hover at the side and judge *his* cheese platter. I'd never signed up for this role. All of my duties were assumed, no negotiation or divvying up of responsibilities, no questions asked.

Later that night, I put Felix to bed. I watched his beautifull face as he fell asleep. But I had the sneaking suspicion that none of his presents were what he wanted, and that the party was not at all what he had asked for.

YOU KNOW HOW people say *success doesn't make you happy*? That's not exactly the math of it. The math of it is that you go through your whole life wanting something called success and being able to blame your shitty moods on the fact that you haven't quite found success and you're quite certain that as soon as you get success you will no longer be in said shitty moods.

Then you make a TV show that people love and win an Emmy and you have that thing you call success and you are more or less exactly as awful as you have always been. You are then forced to look in the mirror and say, "I'm in a shitty mood sometimes and it just is."

It's the same with relationships.

One would think that as soon as you get rid of the supposedly offending partner, the man who doesn't understand the ways his male privilege creates an ether of Other for you to live in, then yes, you can start to enjoy life. Wrong. Once you get rid of the annoying partner, you can't blame your moods on your annoying partner. You put on *Real Housewives* and you look around your TV room and now you have no one, nothing, not one thing to blame. There is nothing obvious to fix. This is a very sad moment.

NIGHTS WERE LONELY now that I was single again, but days were cranking forth. I felt inflated with purpose. Directing was so easy. It felt like my birthright. I had such grief over the wasted years, that I had always believed the hype, the legends about who got to be filmmakers. If you didn't grow up in that way, Super 8 in your hand, obsessed with what you could make the camera do, well, forget it.

How did men just keep taking up space as the default storytellers? Never mind that women are *always* telling stories, about their lives and their best friends' lives, in everyday conversation. But they made us believe that's not real story. And as girls, we were always playing dolls. Was that real story? You realize, when you make a movie, that you've been doing this your whole life. Filmmaking is dolls.

Why were there so many times that I told cis men I was ready to direct and was denied? I asked for gigs, I demanded, I negotiated, I tried to include it in my contracts:

Could I please direct an episode? Every single one of them said no—you're not ready.

Men could arch toward their dream of being designated geniuses, with so much unpaid and unnamed help from wives and mothers and assistants who get their shine from their proximity to the genius. Assisting in creating this ambient sense of belonging that men move through the world with.

Sometimes I tripped on the math: I had finally made it, had this TV show and all of this power, and yet still, I lived in the constant fear that the show would say too much. I had to fight the urge to shrink from the exposure of all of these people knowing too much, thinking that I was too much.

Then I would think about Giancarlo Stanton. He played for the Miami Marlins and he had just gotten a $325 *million* contract for three years and he's just one guy, one I've never heard of, on a team I've barely heard of. I used the idea of him to remind myself that I was nowhere near too big yet. I would multiply the scope of his salary potential atop all of the baseball players, at least twenty-five guys on a team, and how many baseball teams are there, thirty?

And not just baseball, but basketball and football and hockey and fucking golf. Okay now we're talking billions upon billions of dollars spent to help men watch men do things of interest to mostly men. The culture offering them exactly what they love all weekend long in the form of professional sports. A whole section just for them about this stuff every day in the newspaper.

How would it be to have things you love surrounding you everywhere?

My favorite sport is feminist arguing. I'd love an Emily Nussbaum versus Lena Dunham face-off, to hear Roxane Gay and bell hooks disagreeing about a nuance around, say, consent through an intersectional lens, and then they get into it with Patrisse Khan Cullors and Linda Sarsour and Susan Stryker, with a couple Glorias—both Steinem and Allred. What if the thing I like—feminist arguing—was on TV all weekend long? Tune in to catch the semi-finals between Janet Mock and Jennifer Finney Boylan? Women wearing jerseys and carrying key chains that had names like Tina Fey and Alicia Garza and Tarana Burke on them?

What if I got to watch this collision of all my very favorite people every Sunday all day at home in my sweatpants with a beer, and my whole family had to watch and cheer with me? What if there were whole shows devoted to cooking in the parking lots of these events—picture Masha Gessen and Jessica Valenti sitting across from each other in folding chairs on a huge field, with close-ups on the jumbotron? And if I didn't want to watch the Gessen-Valenti game at home I could walk into a bar and there would be a bunch of women watching it. And then when the matches weren't on TV, I'd be clicking away, entering names into an Excel spreadsheet where I'd be *betting* on fantasy feminist arguing? Now *this* would be privilege. And although I had the empire of a TV show, I could see that even my grandest possible achievement would be valued less than a couple of baseball players doing one afternoon's work.

Sometimes I trip on how all women are anxious and spinning trying to survive patriarchy, and I wonder what would happen if we all turned off our cellphones to stare at the moon together. Could we change the world in an instant?

As we got into Season Three, I wanted to do all I could to give people more control. I rewrote people's scripts less, and gave writers leadership roles in connection with their directors. I told them to head off and make the best art they could together out of their episode, and to let me know if they needed me. I got involved only when there was conflict that couldn't be resolved, but that happened less and less frequently as time went on.

We began to live inside the rules of our Topple production company principles, those culture-building rules that we'd modeled on the leadership principles created by Amazon. We referred to them often: Make things happen without anger or punishment, no shit hitting the fan, no throwing people under the bus. Be chill.

Jeffrey, somehow, never got this. I never saw it happen; he would do it only when I left. But the set was often influenced by a weather system known as Jeffrey's possible moods. He was a package of raw nerves threatening to unravel in pain and anger. This is what made him such a beautiful actor to watch. You are watching that undulation. But when the cameras weren't rolling it was real life. Sometimes I would get calls from the set. *You better get here. Jeffrey needs you.* It was like being a mom. Or a daughter whose life depended on stopping Dad from raging.

WHEN I WAS a kid we never went to temple, and as a young adult I couldn't even tell you when Yom Kippur was. But when Johnny and I had Isaac, we sent him to a Jewish school. Shortly after, I was randomly invited to attend Reboot, a think tank for restless but ambitious young Jews, and that kicked off a side hustle where I weaved my improv comedy

showmanship into new Jewish community events and ritu-
als. I cofounded an organization called East Side Jews, with
some friends from Reboot and parents from the Silverlake
JCC, where Felix went to preschool. We did weird events
with revolving clergy and cool bands at the L.A. River on
Rosh Hashanah, and made Havdalah in a store on a rainy
night with French fries and spices and a porn star.

But I still didn't have a temple.

Back when Bruce and I were still married, I was talking
to his sister, Tracy. We complained about the fact that there
were none of those really brilliant, charismatic rabbis in
Los Angeles. We did some asking around and found a rabbi
named Mordecai Finley. He had an independent, interde-
nominational, and vaguely Kabbalistic-adjacent congrega-
tion that held High Holiday services in a big old theater in
Koreatown. It was one of the first traditions Bruce and I
started together as a couple, and I was instantly hooked.

Rabbi Finley had a way of talking about the ten days between Rosh Hashanah and Yom Kippur as a yearly purge,
a sabbath of the year, a time when you could sit in the pew
and meditate on the things you wanted to change. You
didn't even have to follow along with the prayer book. It was
about dedicating consistent and repeated energy toward re-
addressing your interior life. The familiar prayers and the
sounds of the violinist playing Kol Nidre coursing through
the room worked a tearful Jewy magic on me.

I could feel things changing.

It was getting nice and cold in Los Angeles in early Oc-
tober, which really made it feel like the High Holidays, the
season change. I liked to get to services early and find a
place to sit on my own.

I paused at the doors to the sanctuary. I wondered if it would be weird if I wore a kippah. No, I did not want to be a man. But I had short hair like a man and in the sea of heads with short hair, my head without a kippah surely stood out.

It felt too vulnerable to be that guy, the lesbian with a kippah; I couldn't do it. If I did, would I be the kind of guy who would need a bobby pin to secure it? I did grab a prayer shawl from the front hall, one of the musty blue and white guest tallits that had probably been in a cardboard box all year. The man next to me showed me how to put it on. Kiss the collar. Flip it behind you. Toss the corners over your shoulders over and over and over again, get comfortable. Fidget with the strings and knots. Bat wings.

Standing and sitting and standing and sitting, I tried to be strong, telling myself to just hold on to who I had been and who I was becoming.

I thought about how Bruce had joined me at temple the first few years we were married, but then in the years that followed, had always wanted to go surfing if he had the day off. I would either go by myself or convince my kids to come with me, or sometimes Faith. I'd look around at the couples, the families, imagining them getting dressed up for temple together. What would it be like to be part of a couple where both people believed in Finley's version of an ultimate authority, a great divine accessed through the metaphor of a sovereign gateway into love, justice, truth, and beauty? Bruce knew I wanted him with me, yet that was never enough reason for him to come. All I wanted was for him to know it mattered to me, so much so that he would never make me ask. There had been no way out, except now there was. I was out. We were divorced.

I thought about how fast everything had happened. Was it really only four short years ago that I'd decided I was done with L.A.? I had wanted out of the TV business, was going to move to Northern California, wear a caftan with no underwear, sit with a cup of coffee in the morning, and self-publish feminist poetry. I made that decision in 2012, just before my parent came out. It was at a rock-bottom moment, when I'd heard that yet another project wasn't getting the green light. I was out of prospects; my savings were completely gone. There were options in flux and interests and attachments; lunches on the books with Dylan McDermott and Dermot Mulroney. I had balls in the air but no money balls.

I'd go to staffing meeting after staffing meeting, and afterward I would get in my car and call my agent. "Yeah, it's not gonna happen on that one, or that one," he'd say. "I'm sorry, I'm crazed. I'll try to figure out what happened soon. I'll call you when all this dies down."

Staffing season did, in fact, die down. It was all over. No job for me. We really were out of money. Stop spending money. Stop.

I was eating Progresso from the cabinet when I got the call that there was one last job prospect, an opening on *Glee*. Like Charlie when he found out the fifth golden ticket was counterfeit, I ran to the candy store to buy one last Wonka Bar! I called Jane Lynch, who had played Carol in *The Real Live Brady Bunch* back in Chicago. I watched twenty episodes and read every last recap. Started dreaming up scenarios for the characters. Went to the meeting. Blasted it out of the water.

By the time I got in my car my agent called.

"They loved you," he said. "The job is yours! Pop the champagne!"

My mom and sister happened to be in town and soon we were all in my kitchen, dancing. *Jill's gonna make it in Hollywood, just like we all always dreamed!* That night we went out to dinner at an actual restaurant.

On Monday I started planning my work outfits and checked in with my agent. He told me that the offer hadn't come in yet but he'd call me as soon as it did. On Tuesday, there was still no call.

"Don't you think you should call them?" I asked.

"I don't chase offers," he said.

On Wednesday I wrote a concerned but calmly worded email about whether or not I should trust my Spidey sense that something was not quite right. *Are you worried?* I emailed him. No answer. By Thursday, I was at the end of my sweaty, sweaty rope. I emailed him one desperate sentence: *IF YOU KNOW SOMETHING PLEASE PUT ME OUT OF MY MISERY.*

The phone rang. It was him, plus another agent.

"So, you were right. The offer's not coming."

"The offer's not coming? What happened?"

"Apparently, they asked around about you, and word came back that you're difficult."

"Difficult? What? Who the *fuck* called me difficult?"

That job offer went away. Things kept going downhill. I spent more and more time googling houses in Shasta. And then I'd gotten the phone call from my parent—the beat change, the left turn.

———

EVERYTHING HAPPENED SO FAST. It felt like the only way to measure it was to count the High Holidays. This was the sixth time I'd sat in those pews since I discovered Rabbi Finley and the third time since that phone call.

And today, now that Bruce and I were divorced, I didn't even know where he was. Maybe out of town with his new girlfriend, or probably surfing; it was no longer my business to get him to do Jewish stuff with me. Next year I would make sure Faith could be in town for the High Holidays. And I would get my kids to come. This had to matter to all of us as a family. That's what you're supposed to do, right? Tell them to come, and they say they won't come, and then you force them to come, and then there you are, in temple, surrounded by your family, and you feel right, right?

It didn't matter that we weren't married anymore; I was still getting disappointed in the exact same ways.

I ran my fingers over the black letters. *Forged in fire*, they said about the words of the Torah. I wanted to get up and leave. Instead I sat there, and tried to let the ancient melodies do their work on me.

12   GO TOWARD IT

A FEW MONTHS AFTER ELLEN TOLD ME SHE HAD CANCER, SHE TOOK A bad turn. She was struggling with the side effects of the chemo and had to change treatments. Even on her most awful days, Ellen is kinder and in a better mood than I am on my best.

I knew we had to believe that she was going to be fine, but I also needed to ask her to tell me everything she wanted me to know. Just in case we didn't have very much time.

In her office, I got out my journal and pen. I wrote furiously like a court stenographer while she spoke.

This is what she said:

1. Know yourself. Your mind is so dynamic and so are your moods. Keep your ear most attuned to your own voice.
2. Don't get swept away. Allow your impulses to enter your mind, but don't chase them right away. Watch them, tolerate them; some stay, some go away. You see something shiny, new, on the water. It's just something bobbing; don't grab on to it like a buoy.

3. Use anxiety for good, not evil.
4. Don't be a grenade thrower. Dial back the incendiary, provocative nature of your personality; it's not in integrity with yourself.
5. Live on a higher level—you can see more of the impact of your words, actions, love.
6. Don't interrupt the flow of necessary movement. Take pleasure in that flow, and get the whole lay of the land—not just the trees in front of you. Learn the phrases "Let me think" and "That's interesting." You never have to answer. The reactive mode is so common to women.
7. Think of listening like letting down your milk to nurture relationships. It's a way of nurturing your own soul—to be giving to people.
8. People who experience high anxiety are juggling whatever it is instead of leaving *it* alone.
9. Don't be a stick. Let your body be welcoming and soft. Let go, be held.

After I finished writing, I looked at the words in my journal. As the divas say, Ellen had *read* me.

"You know I'm not there, right? I'm not in the journal?" she said.

"I guess?"

"I'm here," she said, pointing to her head, meaning my head. "You can just talk to me anytime. You already know what I would say about everything."

I tried not to cry.

I cried.

I can't live without you, I thought.

Over the next few weeks, Ellen continued to tell me the truth rather than wait for me to figure it out. I was so afraid that every session would be the last time I saw her that I made full afternoons out of driving west to see her. I now knew what beauty and intimacy were: this thing we had for one or two hours when she could fit me in between doctor's appointments.

In exploring those deepest layers of meaning that Ellen was helping me find, I tried to make Season Three into a spiritual quest for the characters as well, allowing them to ask questions about duality and wholeness, about knowing yourself and loneliness.

Maura starts out the season ticking off the list of everything she's "gotten." She's out of the closet, has a great house, has love, but she still doesn't feel better. Raquel is in a forest, trying to write a Passover sermon, talking about that feeling of being chased. What is it that's coming for me? An unanswered email or my own consciousness? Ali ran around in that same forest, that Garden of Eden, during her goddess vision quests under nitrous at the dentist.

If Season Two was about epigenetic inheritance and trauma, Season Three put us in the direct line of it. We saw young Maura fighting to survive her abusive grandfather. Our Lady J wrote an episode that rose directly from her memories of being gendered as a boy in school sports activities, a game of Red Rover gone wrong. There's a climactic episode set in 1950s Boyle Heights where Maura's grandfather finds her cross-dressing in an air-raid shelter. We wrote it to honor Carrie's stories. It was her underground space alone, to be herself, or to be neither, or both.

We had hired a trans actress named Sophia Grace

Giannamore to play young Maura. By this time, our Trans-firmative Action Program was vibrant and healthy. Van moved from her job in Costumes to become Jeffrey's assistant. There were so many trans actresses on the show in some capacity that we started to feel like maybe we had made up for the misstep of casting Jeffrey. Alexandra Billings and Trace Lysette now made recurring appearances, Van Barnes and Our Lady J had occasional speaking roles, and we'd written a role for Alexandra Grey, whom we'd met at a Trans Pride casting event held yearly at the LGBT center. She'd grown up in foster care in Chicago, was kicked out of her house when she came out as trans, and had come to L.A. to dream the dream. Now she was part of our family. There were trans people in every department, and the language and culture of centering and normalizing transness was sewn into everything.

IN JANUARY I got a call that Isaac's paternal grandmother, Dorothy, had slipped and fallen getting out of the tub. The next day, she told Johnny that she was fine, but that her head hurt a little. They took her to the doctor and found a brain bleed. When she was brought into the ICU, they were told she wasn't going to make it.

Before I could process the news that her death was imminent, I did my usual avoiding of the feelings. I freaked about the timing, fretting over the fact that Sundance was coming up and I was supposed to be on a panel and premiere a web series. I was certain the funeral was going to end up being on the same day and that I would have to make a choice.

I pulled out Ellen's list.

I thought about how I needed to live on a higher level in order to understand the impact of my words and actions. If I took Isaac to Virginia for Dorothy's funeral, that would be acting out of awareness, a way to love and support Isaac, to bring our family closer together.

Later that day, I read a review of *Transparent* that, like many other reviews, said something like:

Look at these poor Pfeffermans. They're all so in need of love. Yet here are these people all around them who love them. I watch them and think, LOOK, right next to you, at your sister or your mother or your father, these people love you so much! Lean on them, open up to them, rest your head on their various bosoms.

This is another weird thing about having your TV or film scripts made. You get instant psychological diagnoses in the guise of reviews. If it was true of the Pfeffermans, it was probably true of the Soloways. Probably true of me.

DOROTHY PASSED AWAY a few days later. Everything in our life was pointing toward this. I had to synthesize Ellen's suggestions into real life. Isaac needed to properly say goodbye to his grandmother. He needed to be with his dad and aunt and cousins. And I needed to be there to support him. Love is an action, love is attention. Even if I am afraid of the consequences of my desire, I shouldn't get that confused with love. We have to love as much as we can, especially when it comes to family. I went toward it.

———

"WE'RE COMING!" I said into the phone, like the kind of person who shows up for things. I bought plane tickets immediately.

But it was January, and the following day the news exploded with breathless blizzard porn: there was a Big One Comin'. This would be a Snowmageddon to end all Snowmageddons; the storm's name was Jonas and it was due to smack into Richmond on Friday. But no problem—I knew how to prioritize important people and love and family. We decided to get out ahead of it, to fly early, on a Thursday. But Jonas decided to fly early, too. Every time we got to a new city there was another five-hour delay; once we had to get off a plane that we'd just boarded because of a malfunctioning latch on a baggage compartment.

We finally made it to the end of our day, just one short flight away from Charlotte. We were sad and sweaty and rumpled and overfull from lemon LUNA bars. But moments after we boarded, the flight was canceled.

We saw people walk-running as we trooped back down the Jetway. Employees were turning signs over and locking up drawers, getting out, going home. The actual airport was closing, like a mall closes at the end of the day.

I waited in a short line with a few last panicky people and finally got to an employee to ask: When this happens, you put people up, right? Normally we would, he said, but there is a big college football game and every hotel room in town is booked.

Isaac and I exchanged looks. A few moments of shock paralyzed us, and we realized we were going to have to rely on our grit, which was something I'd never taught him how to do. Instead, we had watched *Ellen* every day at three-thirty when he got home from school. We gathered our luggage and a shopping bag filled with leftover ribs and two Caesars and headed down the escalators to the Great Hall of Car Rentals.

I didn't want to drive five hours into the night with a storm on our asses, but we had no choice. There was a definite vibe that they would run out of rental cars at any minute, so we split up, one of us at Hertz and the other at Alamo. I made a panicky call to some friends who live in South Carolina and asked how far away they were. Three hours in the opposite direction. *Maybe we should drive there,* I thought. It was closer and away from the storm. But we would miss the memorial. And I would be walking backward, back down the steps of the high dive.

As I waited, I saw the Munchian *Scream* faces of people being turned away from Hertz and Alamo.

There were: NO. MORE. CARS.

What would happen? Would we all sleep in that hall together on our luggage?

A man approached.

"Do you need a ride to Richmond?" He nodded his head in the direction of two other men in off-brand polos and khakis, company-logo fleece pullovers. "My friends and I are renting a car; want to come?"

Isaac and I exchanged a hundred psychic thoughts in an instant: *Is this man safe or a serial killer? Do we want to ride for five hours with strangers? This could be a good story. But it could also end in our deaths. Did all three of those men want to rape us? What kind of car did they have? Could they tell by looking at us that we were Jewish? That I was somewhat of a leader in the Jewish community? Did they know I now got my hair cut at the barbershop? That I had sex with women? That I myself wasn't even sure if I was totally still a woman? And what about our white privilege? This is so unfair—they never would have offered us a ride if we weren't white. Was that enough of a reason to not accept it?*

Our eyes flashed some sort of *knowing* back and forth. I decided it meant that I had Isaac's permission. I said yes.

As we walked to the car they introduced themselves—Donnie, Keith, and Sean. In the dark of the underground garage, we got in the way, way back of their van. Keith stayed outside of the car and helped Donnie back up. It was company policy.

Once we started driving, they had to introduce themselves many more times because we kept getting texts from our friends:

> —GET THEIR NAMES!
> —GET THEIR LAST NAMES!
> —GET PICTURES OF THEIR DRIVER'S LICENSES!
> —GET PICTURES OF THE LICENSE PLATE!

Donnie was a kindly, white-haired grandfather type from Virginia who lived not too far from where Isaac's cousins lived in Oilville. Sean was younger, maybe in his fifties, with the goatee all men of a certain region wear. And they were laughing because it would have been Keith's first time on an airplane.

"Can you believe it? Keith was so nervous to fly, and we

made fun of him," they told us. "Nothing ever goes wrong, but look here."

They showed us photos on Sean's iPad of the conference they had just been to. They all worked for Dominion Energy. We told them that Isaac's uncle Owen used to work for Dominion, and through the power of the hail-fellow-well-met fraternity of coworkers, everyone's shoulders relaxed. The five-hour ride went so much faster than we could have imagined. Sean had a Doppler app, and we stayed about forty miles ahead of the storm. Isaac and I texted each other comic insights about how it felt to be in the back of their van.

Things were chatty until the impending presidential primary came up. Their votes were spread among Trump, Romney, and Cruz. Each one of them told at least a half-hour story about the details of their life and work. I wondered if they would ask what I did. They didn't.

Then at some point, knowing that we lived in L.A., they asked what famous people we knew. I said I had met a couple in my day, and that finally made Keith ask if I had a job, and when I told them what I did, they asked for the name of the TV show.

Isaac and I looked at each other. We were almost to Richmond and we were still alive. Why risk it? But I believe in love, and so I told them.

"It's called *Transparent*."

They hadn't heard of it.

"It's on Amazon."

"Oh, you can watch TV on Amazon?"

"Yup."

"What's it about?"

"It's about a family where the father comes out as trans."
Silence.

"What would make you come up with an idea like that?"
A little more silence.

"Oh, my father is trans."

Silence for about fifteen full minutes, not even a word about the Doppler.

Then as we got closer to Oilville, conversation started to bubble up again. Maybe because we all knew that soon we would be free of one another. They had probably started texting each other that Isaac and I were going to rape and kill them.

We dropped Keith and Sean at the Richmond airport to get their cars, and Donnie drove us the rest of the way. By the time we arrived at Isaac's cousins' house as the sun was coming up, I felt a huge surge of love for Donnie and the kind of beautiful Republican Man that he was, the kind who drives through the night with a storm on his ass and takes strangers with him.

Isaac and I crept into the house. Everyone was still sleeping. But soon everyone awoke, four cousins plus a boy-friend. The storm hit, dropping sheets and sheets and sheets of white. Johnny had thought to bring over an electric guitar and a couple of drums and some sound equipment. He put amps and speakers in the living room near the piano. His teenage nephews wandered around in their PJs, picking up the guitar to strum it.

Isaac got behind the drum set and started playing. He made a face when he was getting into the music, like an imitation of a guy who's oh-so-deep in the feelings of the music, this face we call "bass face," a snarling *oomph oomph* feeling of getting lost in joy.

We'd had a drum set at our house when Isaac was little, and he took lessons with a percussionist named Marcus. He got bored, and I didn't push him. When Bruce entered our lives, he and Isaac took turns on the drum set. Bruce helped him learn. People would come over and we would have jam sessions, Faith on the piano, Isaac or Bruce on the drums.

They had been so connected those first couple of years, Isaac and Bruce. But when Felix was born, Bruce wanted to focus only on him. Isaac stopped playing the drums again. Bruce had stopped playing the drums unless he was filled with emotion. Like when all four of us were getting ready to go out, and someone was running late, and instead of yelling for us to hurry, Bruce used to get on the drums and pound out an anthem to his frustration.

In Isaac's cousins' house in Virginia, with the snow falling everywhere outside, Isaac used the brushes gently on the cymbals, leading the song with his mellow rhythmic Isaac ways. His cousins Jake and Zack folded in, and his grandpa John did his little dance, the one where he holds his paws up and shakes his hips a little. It was all so beautiful.

Later we bundled up in their thick hunting camo, went outside, and flopped ourselves into the snow. We pretended to be in *The Revenant,* crawling around looking for a horse to hide inside of to keep warm. There was so much ice in the creek, floes of it.

The neighbors came over on their four-wheeler. They had cold red faces and mirrored sunglasses and Bloody Mary mix. We all started drinking. Hours and hours passed. Johnny is a really good cook. I was his sous chef as he made a delicious stone stew with things from the cabinet that weren't really food by themselves. The cousins hadn't gone to the store to stock up before Jonas. They weren't Jewish.

We ran out of booze. Jen and I got on the back of the four-wheeler and went a half mile or so through the snow back to the neighbors' house. Once we got there, we agreed that we should bring every last drop of booze in their house back with us. We loaded all of it into a cardboard box that I held in my lap as the four-wheeler carved through the snow. Soon it was late afternoon, and things became like Montessori for adults. Folks were alternately jamming, drinking, cooking, eating—drifty and lazy, time changed shape. We could be here forever. Just us would be enough. There was the land and whatever was in the cupboard.

We started a Snow Jam Cult and gathered in a circle and talked about our memories of Dorothy. Isaac and I slept on air mattresses. The day and a half turned into two and a half days and felt like a week.

The storm passed, and I made it to Sundance in time for whatever I needed to be there for, and Isaac made it back to school. Every step of the way there had been signs that we should turn around, go back, run away from the hard path. But we had stayed the course together, and remembered and honored Isaac's grandmother.

I AM / I WANT

WAS STARTING TO FEEL MORE COMFORTABLE IN THE SINGLE LIFE. Less lonely. More aware that spending time alone was what I needed.

In the old days, when I was in my twenties and writing screenplays, I would wake up and write for a half hour every morning. Scott Silver, the screenwriter who wrote *8 Mile*, once told me: *Your head is filled with inspiration during the first thirty minutes of the day. Don't lose it. Don't even make coffee. It's all there. Just start.*

One morning while we were shooting Season Three, I woke up with a Zen koan in my head:

> *I want / I'm not*
> *I am / I want*

As I lay in bed I thought about what it meant. *I want / I'm not* is how I had always lived my life. *Wanting* immediately named a lack, a deficit proven by the evidence that if I wanted something, I didn't already have it. But this new version began with *I am*, meaning that the *want* was an original expression of my resting state. I suddenly understood *wanting* as a powerful, even dignified activity rather than an expression of need.

I wondered if this was the way white cis hetero men woke up every day, with *I am* as their first thought.

Is this what it feels like to be a man, or is this what it feels like to be an artist?

Still in bed, I grabbed a notebook. I was reminded of what it felt like to fall in love with Eileen, how I'd reach for paper to write it all down, what I admired about her. I'd loved how she valued her own mind, her abstract connections, her self-respect, and how she created for the sake of it, not the possible financial value. I wanted to hold space for my own thoughts.

I made a list for myself. There had to be principles to live by. Not just Ellen's, but also my own. What did I want? And how was I going to get it?

This is what I wrote:

1. Go on a walk every morning. Be in the world with your mind. Let the thoughts move through. Prioritize this over everything—it's your meditation.
2. Now that you have your oxygen mask adjusted, turn to your children. They are next. Then your family. Your sister, your parents, your extended family.
3. Then your job. Work is not love. Love is love.
4. Breathe. Slowly.
5. Don't rush into limerence. Take your time. See how people treat you. Concocting a connection is not the same thing as a connection.

6. Invasiveness is not the same as intimacy.
7. Impulse is not the same as instinct.
8. When you don't know what to do, remind yourself that you have a body and check in with what your body wants. It's okay to want something, and it's also okay to not want something.
9. You're not in trouble and you haven't done anything wrong.

The last one is a mantra that I repeat in my mind when it wants to zoom into spirals of self-critique. I wanted to stop searching for my own fuck-ups, to stop awaiting emails and texts to come along to force me backward to confirm that I had indeed done something wrong. I was like a trail horse that knew only one way back to the stable. My old habits were keeping me from being present. I had to find a way to regularly remind myself that everything was okay.

Life started to feel easier, and my relationships became more stable. Bruce and I were getting along really well. We threw a high school graduation party for Isaac and sent him off to college. He made the transition with great power and beautiful calm.

Felix seemed to relax a little, no longer caught in that staticky space between two people who didn't quite know how to be whole yet and didn't know how to say that. Without the projection where Bruce was watching me parent and I was watching Bruce watching me parent, and vice versa, we could actually be there to parent him, admire him, inspire him, and be inspired by him. Bruce and I were able to have good conversations about Felix's needs instead of avoiding communication. Felix seemed to like being able to have each parent to himself for a week. He was growing into an incredibly beautiful and self-aware kid. He had Bruce's physical confidence and was starting to skateboard and take chances. His brilliance astounded me.

That spring, Pidgeon Pagonis, an intersex activist I'd met at our "Champions of Change" White House event, came to visit L.A. They were doing activist work and also playing a small role in an episode, at the suicide help line where Maura worked. I offered them a room in my house. In anticipating their arrival, I started to see the ways that I had always used gender as a tool to organize my behavior.

If "she" were a dyke or a cis chick from Chicago, I'd treat her one way: *Hey, hang out up in my room with me; come out with all of us on a girls' night.*

If "he" were a straight cis man, visiting: *Yeah, so put your stuff in the guest room—hey, do you wanna go surfing with Bruce?*

If "he" were a gay man, I'd introduce him to my single gay friends, and give him a key in case he wanted to go down to Akbar and dance and stay out late.

But Pidgeon couldn't be put into any category. It felt like a devotional act, to choose *neither* and *both* in *every moment,* a little brain pause of awareness, which felt like respect and appreciation. I'd heard about *theybies,* kids whose parents are going as long as possible without naming a gender. How beautiful that could be. To catch yourself before calling your baby a "strong little man" or a "pretty little girl." To respond to tears as tears and not as signs of betrayal to particular expectations. How would it be if everybody saw pure soul before gender? I had been thinking about identifying as nonbinary for a while now and it felt like time.

The promise of identifying as nonbinary felt like the promise of being held in a moment. Hovering in that space when you go through a revolving door and stop halfway through and there you are, not out or in, just in between. And if time froze, or if the revolving door got jammed for a second, right there, well, you could stay there, surrounded by glass, and see the busy inside of the warm yellow perfume of Marshall Field's and the snowy blue cold Chicago street. Not having to be in or out yet. Not having to choose.

WE HAVE THIS TRADITION when we shoot called "Box." Someone puts an apple box in the center of the floor. People call out "Box, box, box" and drift in from all areas of the set. We spend fifteen or twenty minutes before the shooting day in collective community, standing in a circle. People stand on the box and tell stories about their kids' sports teams or what's going on with their wives. Sometimes it's voluntary and sometimes people are tapped.

As a leader, I was in awe of the power of the Box: what it means to have the opportunity to create culture for a whole group of people from that circle. I started to think about getting on the Box one day and coming out as nonbinary at work. This was such a safe space, but I still felt my heart pounding and my cheeks flush as I imagined saying it. Saying *I am* or *I think I am* or *I might be* in front of a group of people.

I also knew I would have to get over the fear of people's hassled feelings—this thing that was for me a delightful course correction might cause straight-up panic in others.

I didn't want people to worry: *What is Jill and will I get in trouble if I get it wrong?*

But this wasn't the real world, this was our world, where lots of people name their pronouns and use new pronouns.

As we gathered I went back and forth in my head. *I'm going to say it. I'm not going to say it. I'm going to say it. I'm not going to say it. Jesus Christ, isn't there already enough attention on you? Isn't this just another attention-getting ploy?*

I decided that if I couldn't say it here, I couldn't say it anywhere.

I got up on the Box. Looked around at the gathered sweet faces.

"So, this is hard for me, and really weird for me," I started. "But I've been wanting to tell you guys that I don't really identify with the word "female," or "woman," and I never have; I mean, I have occasionally, but mostly have found it confusing. So . . ."

I started to cry a little. Then wiped the tears away. Gathered myself.

"I am starting to think of myself as nonbinary. And you don't have to get my pronouns right. I don't even get them right. If you do, that's great. Anyway, I just wanted to tell you all."

I stepped off, my heart jumping.

MIDSEASON, WE ALL gathered again to watch the Emmy nominations together, and when they named our show we couldn't believe we were still in it. A few months later, back to awards week and everything that goes with it. I spent less time figuring out my clothes this time around. I went to the ceremony with Isaac again; we were making it a thing.

When I heard my name called for the directing award, I galloped up onto the stage. Hillary was about to be elected president and I was so glad that the world was finally catching up with feminism that I ended my speech by calling out "Topple the patriarchy!"

It had been about four years since my parent had come out as trans. My journey had started with panic in response to the initial phone call—the shame, the urge to run, then the need to solve it all by making art out of it, the characters and scenes emerging in my mind. Now the show had not just changed me and our family, but also the world.

According to various blogs, I actually yelled "Topple the patriarchy!" twice. I must have been in an Emmy fugue because I don't remember this. Maybe my new *I am / I want* revelation allowed me to say exactly what I wanted, without worrying what people would think of me.

Afterward I went backstage and turned in my fake Emmy for my real Emmy. By now I knew the ropes. McDonald's wasn't sponsoring that year so there were no salty hot French fries.

I used my few minutes with the press corps to assert that Trump was evil incarnate. A few days before I had seen a video of him calling Rosie O'Donnell a pig to an auditorium full of laughing and cheering people and watched it go viral. And it wasn't just about women—it was about everything. His rhetoric about the border wall, his xenophobia, his white supremacy. I knew fascism when I saw it. I wondered if there was a simple way for me to say something that would wake up just a few more people so that they could make the connection before the election.

About a month later, an audiotape was released of Trump saying stuff like "big phony tits / I just start kissing them / Just kiss / they let you do it / grab 'em by the pussy."

I just *knew* that it was absolutely all over for him.

And then, a month later, America elected him anyway.

A shadow of a black balloon the size of the planet floated over us. There was so much sadness and so much rage that we couldn't take him down. We thought we had power, but no, actually, we were this thing—this Other Thing called Women, and we could be silenced, disregarded, with a vote.

We did the only thing we knew how to do: work.

I was excited about our story for Sarah. In an earlier season, she left her husband when she came out as gay. But they'd drifted back into an arrangement where they were living together and getting their needs filled by others, in boundaried pods, nonintegrated sexploitations. We wanted to tell a story about multiplicity by putting Sarah and Len on a poly path with an old friend, a teacher from their kid's preschool. The character's name was Lila and she was played by Alia Shawkat.

Len and Sarah contemplated whether they could bring a third person into their love story. How would that work, exactly? I was really moved when we filmed one scene in particular, a twenty-two-minute ramble where Sarah, Len, and Lila get together to look at a legal contract, and then decide to extend their afternoon by a few hours. Soon there's a revelation that Lila and Sarah had met at a sex addicts' meeting. Len gets angry. Lila comes to Sarah's defense. After defending her, Lila says she likes to sleep with couples, talking in a way meant to turn on both Len and Sarah. Sarah and Lila kiss., Len takes control and narrates. Sarah tells him to stop narrating; she wants to be the narrator. The three of them have sex.

I realized as we were filming that each and every one of the beat changes was a move through another gauntlet of consent. There were a lot of nonverbal cues, unspoken ways that all three let one another know they wanted to be there.

It was so exciting to watch the scene come together in the rough cut and see these beat changes slow moments down to ascertain whether or not consent was happening. I thought about all the movies that cut away from first kiss to moments later, the couple going at it in an abstract, sporty manner. Or even worse, that couple post-sex, sheets around their waists. This was the male gaze editing out not only our desire but also our consent. Training us all to believe that our consent either isn't interesting or isn't necessary. I realized that one of the things we had been doing on the show over the years was showing what female consent looks like.

Season Four also has a story about Josh going to a twelve-step meeting and admitting to himself that the thing he thought of as sex with Rita was actually rape. He was an adolescent and she was an adult, and he couldn't have meaningfully consented. Someone in his support group says, "Erection is not consent," and he lights up. *This is me,* he thinks. Those four words illuminate something about his shame.

In addition to exploring these themes surrounding consent, we decided to take the Pfeffermans to Israel. We had always known that one day they would have to hit the Promised Land in a tour bus. "Next Year in Jerusalem" is the cry that Jewish families repeat yearly at Seders, and we were no different.

As we started to write the Israel story line, word got out among our queer academic friends. Sarah Schulman, an activist and writer whose books include *Israel/Palestine and the Queer International* and *Conflict Is Not Abuse*, emailed me. She, and many in our extended queer family, support the Palestinian-led boycott. *Transparent* shooting and spending there would be in opposition to their ideals.

"But the whole season is about Israel," I told Sarah. "We have to shoot there."

I thought about the ways that Werner Herzog and Andrea Arnold talked about the camera as a giant cornucopia, as a tsunami or a vacuum that goes places and gobbles everything up. Shooting on fake sets instead of on location made me feel not like the warrior adventurer I wanted to be. But I couldn't imagine ignoring or making enemies out of trans activists who had been my allies for so many years.

Soon after the phone call, we received a letter from Sarah signed by many trans activists involved in the Boycott, Divestment, and Sanctions movement. They insisted that *Transparent* consider the boycott and cancel plans to shoot on location in Israel. We had a decision to make and it had to be made fast.

Ugh. I was so annoyed. How did I get stuck in this very narrow place of being forced to choose?

Sarah connected me with folks involved in the movement for liberation of the Palestinian people. Artists like

Eve Ensler, James Schamus, and Tony Kushner, plus activists from Jewish Voices for Peace.

"No matter what you do," Tony Kushner told me, "you're stepping in it. You're going to make enemies. Tread carefully."

I spoke to filmmaker Amber Fares, who was from a Muslim family in Toronto, and who had spent a lot of time living and working in Palestine when she made a documentary about female race car drivers living in the West Bank. She told me about spending time with American Jews, and in particular how it felt to see them encounter the West Bank, to watch their privilege peel away.

I thought more and more about how I wanted to have my story peeled away.

"This is bigger than you, Jill," Sarah Schulman said. "You're not going to solve the Middle East crisis with a TV show."

She clearly did not know me. I don't have a lot of things in common with Jared Kushner, but low-grade Jerusalem Syndrome might be one. Maybe I needed to send her the Thanksgiving Paris Manifesto in which Eileen and I created a call to action for people to gather at the walls of the Old City and protect it as a holy place for a multiplicity of many religions—the murdered goddess, the erased divine feminine.

I thought and thought about creating a TV family–shaped delegation to the Promised Land in the hopes that our presence there could set off a chain of events that would lead to the patriarchy toppling. But saying "intersectional power movement" to anyone who would listen was not the same as pushing myself to live in the true uncomfortable zones. The conversations I had with the activists made me see how the otherization inherent in the moral argument for the occupation matches how patriarchy and white supremacy operate. Traveling to Israel and spending money there would have been seen by our queer siblings in the interconnected liberation movements as crossing the boycott, and we just couldn't do that.

Instead, we re-created the Dead Sea in the tank at Universal Studios. I directed that day while floating on two noodles. Felix came to work with me and joined me in the water as I paddled over to the actors to chat and give feedback as they sang songs from *Jesus Christ Superstar.* We made a fake Wailing Wall on the Paramount lot. We brought in background artists who looked like tourists and Haredim. We shoved our little rolled-up holy paper wishes into the cracks, conflating the TV show with our lives, as always. It was a holy scene being shot on a holy day so Jimmy Frohna, who was directing that episode, invited Susan Goldberg, one of our rabbi consultants, to come to bless the set.

But once we finished shooting, I was still feeling a really strong urge to travel to Israel. Maybe if we didn't bring the whole crew and spend hundreds of thousands of dollars our activist siblings wouldn't be alarmed. A few weeks later, Jimmy and I flew there together. We used a small splinter crew to shoot B-roll. Amber met us in Israel and shot footage in Ramallah. Jimmy and I shot in Tel Aviv, Jerusalem, and the Dead Sea. No actors. Just us.

Things had changed since Jimmy and I had made *Afternoon Delight.* There were so many dreams that had driven us, and now they were realized. The roiling hunger we had felt when we first met had subsided, but it was nice to wander the city together.

In a crazy coincidence, Eileen also happened to be in Israel. She was reading at PalFest, a literary festival that brought lauded international writers on a tour of the occupied territories. Amber rented a car so she and I could explore the West Bank and see Eileen read poetry. We crossed over the Qalandia checkpoint that we had heard so much about. It was much like the one we'd built on set. On the other side little boys sold us fidget spinners. I bought one to take back to Felix.

People were on high alert. Ramadan was about to start. Trump was coming for his first visit. Twenty-five imprisoned men were on day thirty of a hunger strike. Five had collapsed the day before.

But early that evening things were chill in Ramallah. Amber and I went to a hipster café filled with artists and filmmakers. As the sun set, Eileen read poetry against a rocky crag behind a building that looked like a small castle on a street up in the hills.

Afterward, Amber and I headed back to the checkpoint to go home to East Jerusalem for the night. The streets started to fill with men wearing black handkerchiefs over their faces and boys with tear gas masks, crowding past murals of revolutionaries with the words RESISTANCE IS NOT TERRORISM. Kids calling out in Arabic darted across the street. Everyone seemed desperate for something big to happen. It was a powder keg. So much unbelievable pain beneath all of the rage.

Suddenly everywhere men were holding sticks, yelling; things were ramping up. There was a fire up ahead, and then multiple fires. The smell of burning tires and burning plastic, the city sky getting hot with smoke that choked our throats.

Amber got the tiniest bit scared. I was even more scared, filled with that familiar sentiment of *Oh God, it's finally happened; it all went horribly wrong and Jilly caused it*. My heart was pounding because the folks at Amazon had told me not to go into Ramallah, and Ellen Silverstein and Rabbi Finley had both given me names of people to call just in case. Write the names on your hand, each had said. But I was certain it was all propaganda, that I would go in to find out for myself.

And now here we were, and it felt like we were in danger. Amber made an ugly five-point turn in our tiny shoe of a car, and we almost hit someone. She wove back through the traffic the wrong way, finding wiggling paths to snake down. I blasted familiar Valerie June songs from my iPhone to calm myself down. We got past the thick clog of demonstrators and left Ramallah through a back entrance a few miles behind the city. Amber's plan was going to be to tell the Israeli guards that she was a journalist and had left her pass in her hotel. Her Canadian accent would make her safe. I told her I could sing some Jewish prayers for the guards so they would know I was a member of the tribe. But when we got to this little quiet border booth, it was unattended. We sailed through and within fifteen minutes I was in my safe bed with the hard white sheets at the American Colony Hotel.

I was overwhelmed with the enormity of my privilege. How Amber and I could slip out, and I could be back in this bed, and soon I would be back on a plane, free to move through the world. Do things like make TV shows and contemplate a million questions about what it meant to want things, knowing that I could have nearly anything if I tried hard enough.

AFTER SHOOTING IN ISRAEL I finally had some time and started to think about dating again. Both Eileen and I were having trouble meeting people, and we thought it might be because we were still a couple according to Google searches. So we held a breakup-processing session onstage at the Hammer Museum in Los Angeles. We wanted to let our 275 mutual fans down in a vaguely entertaining way. We had met on a panel, fallen in love on a stage, so it seemed fitting to announce our breakup officially, then postmortem it on a panel of two. We admitted that we both probably felt most comfortable on panels. She observed that in anticipating our connection, I had created a character for myself, a character custom-designed to appeal to her. But doesn't everyone invent a version of themselves for future lovers upon meeting them? Changing for someone isn't intrinsically bad, if you pick right. Right?

Six months had passed since our announced breakup, and I wanted to be that *I am* person, the one who believes it's okay to want things. I kept thinking the person I wanted to date would come knocking at my door, but she didn't. I told my friends that I wanted to date someone femme, thinking that if I said it out loud maybe I could manifest this person. I finally met her, through friends one night at Outfest. Her name was Lauren and she was way too young. She was only thirty, but other than that, well, we went from talking about movies we liked to telling each other what we were up to throughout the day to sending the last text before bed without thinking twice about it.

I started to inhale this new thing, the pull of the masculine-feminine dynamic again, but now from a different side. As the butch, I felt powerful and handsome, freed of the life sentence of daring to age while female. I felt young. Susan Sontag said:

> *The great advantage men have is that our culture allows two standards of male beauty: the boy and the man . . . Men are able to accept themselves under another standard of good looks—heavier, rougher, more thickly built. . . . There is no equivalent of this second standard for women, every wrinkle, every line, every grey hair, a defeat.*

The more masculine I felt, the more it seemed I was no longer being looked at. Now I was the looker. The shyer she was, the better it was for me, the more I got to perform, to make her smile, giggle, relax. I finally got it. I understood men, how their desire felt original and like the necessary launching of action. All flirting is the slow gaining of consent. The scrutinizing for signals. Can I get closer? Closer? Can I come in? Ah. This is why straight men are so confused.

Rising into an idealized version of myself reminded me that no one ever really falls in love with anyone else. Instead they always fall in love with the version of themselves that they imagine the adored is looking for. Mild to moderate limerence whipped us into a dream of ourselves. We went to SXSW, where I was delivering a keynote speech. I pretended we were John and Yoko. I loved holding her hand backstage. Even though we were in the tiniest room of a janky old Austin hotel, it was heaven. Or like we were in a movie. Feeling like I was in a movie had become the closest I could come to feeling happy.

Lauren saw and longed for all parts of me—the feminist thinker and Joey, the stupid Long Island handsy dude that I sometimes embodied. She was both a brilliant filmmaker and a fake mafia princess; I could waffle back and forth from Jill to some bro named Joey, and in that space become whoever it was I wanted to be.

I saw Valentine's Day coming around the bend and realized there was something different about it now. That dread I'd had my entire life, of how dumb you feel when you don't have a partner, and then that quadruple dumb awful feeling when your partner simply refuses to jump in, or aggressively gets everything totally wrong.

All I'd ever wanted was for Bruce to make it special—to make a plan, make a reservation, make it beautiful. This was something he could not do. The selfless giving of a lovely, romantic gift was still on his to-do list of learning when we were together. Other men, not just Bruce, got it wrong. Wrong restaurant. Not being creative. Giving in to the popular notion that it's a stupid holiday. Of course it's a stupid holiday. Their dumb excuses: *I wouldn't know how to give you what you want.* Just like my dad saying I wouldn't let him teach me how to ride a bike.

But now it was all different.

When I started dating women, dating butches was more or less like dating men, except for the part where they were interested in what I had to say. With Lauren, though, I could give her everything—I could selflessly arrange dates and want her to want things, and there was no scorecard. I actually wanted her to be happy. It was a straight line between her happiness and my desire—no curveballs, no resentment. I wasn't waiting for her to not take care of me so I could be secretly pissed. I wasn't trying to figure out how to make her *want* to take care of me.

I had to work on Valentine's Day, but I had a few hours free in the middle of the day for a longish lunch. We met up at a special secret place. I gave her presents—the best lingerie, plus chocolate just in case she was like me and could find a problem with anything. We had the best sex, which we were really good at. Spooned, took a nap. Went back to work.

That night we also went out to dinner. I had made a reservation. At the right place. She needed to give me no hints. I knew how to get it all right—just to prove to myself that it wasn't that hard to give her something so that she could look at her holiday and say it was perfect.

I went from silently resenting that no one could get it perfect to taking on the whole of perfection.

Those Beyoncé lyrics, *If I were a boy / I'd listen to her / I swear I'd be a better man.* We were now inside of that action plan, two women doing it all differently, just for each other. A door opened like an escape room to a new planet. This new planet that was made for me, and waiting for me all this time—queerness.

BACK WHEN SARAH GUBBINS and I went crazy for Chris Kraus's *I Love Dick*, we'd gotten Amazon to secure the rights to the book. Sarah started writing a pilot, and we'd turned the script in just as Season Three of *Transparent* was getting going. We were elated when Amazon asked us to make a series of it; a production slot had opened up and they wanted to slide it into their schedule superfast if I had the stamina to get another show off the ground.

Did I have the stamina?

No.

Okay, fine, maybe I did have the stamina. But where was it coming from? My ambition only seemed to grow with success. I was feeling like I could do it all. I felt so driven to make *I Love Dick*. Mostly, I couldn't believe I *could* make it, so if they would let me, I had to. This show that was so feminist, so radical, it had the most idiotic name that the average person would think was about loving dick, but it was actually about a woman finding her voice.

I Love Dick was different from anything I'd made before. Even the somewhat experimental subject matter of *Transparent* hewed to certain shapes and velocities, because it was a family show, a salute to *All in the Family* and *Family* and *Eight Is Enough* and *thirtysomething*. *I Love Dick* was different in that it used the form of television for its own purposes. For revolution.

We spent months filming in Marfa, Texas. Going back and forth from L.A. Bringing the writers on research trips. Heading out again with Kevin Bacon and Kathryn Hahn. Eileen was living there and introduced us to everyone; we were like the Hollywood circus coming to town. We all stayed in one hotel; there was only ever one thing going on in a night. We would all walk together to the art gallery. They're serving Ranch Water, some tequila gin–fizz concotion they only make in Marfa. Every single one of us is drinking Ranch Water every night. Now the art opening is ending, all twenty of us walk lawless and laughing down the street carrying our cups to the grilled cheese place and sit in the back and eat together. There is no feeling like *I should be somewhere else*. Everyone was there. Even Isaac and Felix were there for part of the scouting and filming. If I couldn't get away from home much—and I didn't really like vacations anyway (I need a bumper sticker that reads: DOWNTIME MAKES ME ANXIOUS)—I was going to take my kids with me as much as possible whenever we went anywhere fun.

Marfa is a small town a few hours outside of El Paso. High-desert cool founded on an expansive dream of an art town created by Donald Judd. Modernists and architects and artists and people with round ochre spectacles have gathered there for decades. Wide-open skies and fat streets, Latinx kids on bikes like small-town America, but Manhattan weirdos wandering here and there, too. Our crew came and moved in and we collaborated with the beauty that was there. The hot white buildings in the midday sun. The train running through town. We employed local people, set up base camp at the high school parking lot, brought in background artists from the neighboring towns, tried not to harm the surroundings while we made this aria against patriarchy. In the edit we wove in art films by all the women who came before. The episodes we shot were a brazen whirl through how it felt to be Chris, to move to this town and fall hard for someone, but realize you're falling for yourself, your voice. To come alive. To give up everything for lust. To feel artistically fulfilled living inside of your lust.

Sometimes when I try to name exactly what's so fun about filmmaking I remember a scene I directed up at Dick's bunkhouse with Kevin and Kathryn. I had this joke that I'd wanted to use my whole life. It's one of those micro-cringe life moments that happens when a really tender man thinks a woman is beautiful and he wants to tell her gently that she has very beautiful breasts, but then the word "breasts" just keeps going. He can't figure out which should be the last *s*. The man is trying to be sweet but finds himself saying *breaststststs*. It came running at me while I was watching this one scene between Dick and Chris, and after I said "cut," I whispered the joke in Kevin's ear: "So hey, what if you just *couldn't* get the *ts* at the end of the word 'breasts' to stop?" He surprised Hahn with it, and I was laughing so hard at the monitor, transported to my teenage living room where Faith and I are laughing hysterically imagining a man with a deep voice trying to be serious about how beautiful someone's breasts are, but the word keeps coming out *breastssssssss* or *breastuses* or just *breaststststs*, the *ts* sound repeating itself like a dripping faucet.

Filmmaking is a hundred moments like this. You have a filing cabinet in your body of everything you've ever wanted to say, and there it was; I had forgotten it. It was probably in a deleted branch of my brain, but then I remembered it again, and it went in the photo album of this day and it will always be there.

I am not the first person to synthesize my experiences into my filmmaking. That's what all artists do. But *I Love Dick* was about exactly that feeling, using your life for your art, and what it costs. It told the story of what Chris Kraus was talking about in her book: the guilt that women feel when they want things. And the way they are blamed from the outset. The chaos it creates for those around you. The choices women are forced to make that men simply never encounter.

When *I Love Dick* was released it struggled to find its audience. It was a feminist show but the name, taken literally, was the opposite of that. When they released it, Amazon put Kevin Bacon out in front. He had a huge fan base, so people checked it out but didn't finish watching the season. The women who found it loved it. It seemed to inspire people to create, too.

When Chris Kraus wrote the book, the literary community had hated it. No one would read it. She had to go through the art world to distribute it. But ten years later, feminists made it their beloved treasure. When we made the first season of *Dick* and it went out into the world, I realized that Chris had written a book about feeling invisible, and that maybe this created an alchemy where the show was destined to not be watched. *I Love Dick* was a scream, a rant, a cry about no one looking. Of not being able to get anyone to look.

There is an episode where the actress India Salvör Menuez, playing Toby, talks about the ways in which she worshipped Dick throughout her childhood, poring over giant glossy art books and dreaming of one day having his attention, his admiration. Then there's a beat change and she looks into the camera and tells Dick, "We are coming for you." It's an absurd statement, especially in Marfa—like, who would dare have the hubris to stare right at Donald Judd, this man whose ideas of what a line is, a man who gave birth to a chunk of art history and also this place. To stare at him and say: "You're going down. Patriarchy is going down." We all kept saying it.

But no one really expected it to happen.

14   OH, FUCK

TWO YEARS AFTER I'D YELLED "TOPPLE THE PATRIARCHY!" ONSTAGE, it all indeed came tumbling down. In fall 2017, Jodi Kantor and Megan Twohey wrote an impeccably researched investigative piece in *The New York Times* about Harvey Weinstein. Their astonishing reporting gave us the whole picture—the large-scale psychic violence of how Harvey gleefully terrified and terrorized women and the payoffs that helped hide and empower him.

I was heading into a weekend conference when I read the story. The previous year at the same conference, I had sidled up next to him at the breakfast buffet to make small talk about whether the sausages or the bacon might be the right choice. I'd wanted to impress him, to be favored by him. As the scope of the news became real, all of us who had been so hypnotized by him were ashamed that we'd contributed to an ecosystem that coalesced around his power.

But mostly I was in shock, paralyzed by how fast everything was moving. Not just Harvey going down, but more and more men. This moment was unlike anything I could have imagined, what Kwame Anthony Appiah calls a moral revolution. In his book *The Honor Code*, Appiah attempts to understand the mood before, during, and after the cultural transitions when outmoded customs such as duels and foot binding suddenly become not okay.

My friends and colleagues were all texting each other.

> —Who's going down next? Send me the shitty men in media list.
> —PROMISE NOT TO SEND IT TO ANYONE!
> —Of course not.
> —HEY, I JUST GOT THE SHITTY MEDIA MEN LIST. I'll send it to you if you promise not to send it to anyone.

We were giddy.

When we got word that Harvey wasn't coming to the conference this year, it was all anyone could talk about. Had we seen this coming? Who was complicit? Women used forums large and small at the event to start talking. The day after the conference, we all returned to L.A., and more and more men were going down. Suddenly, it seemed like it was *every* man. We felt the dam breaking. Women were coming together, hovering over the assignment desks of one another's websites and newspapers. It was like the Federalist Papers but it was the Feminist Papers, and we were the dudes in *Hamilton*, writing like we were running out of time. Bill Cosby and Roger Ailes and Bill O'Reilly and Charlie Rose, Al Franken and, wait, even Chuck Close? And Louis C.K. All had been named as alleged transgressors.

Over the years I had gotten calls from journalists working on the Louis C.K. story. They had asked me about the women he'd jerked off in front of. *Jill, do you know anyone who would go on the record?* But no one would speak. We were all too scared. Nobody wanted to be the one you could point to and say, *She ruined this guy's career.* The whisper network had been a quiet place where you said things to your friends at dinner parties. Women didn't speak up because it wasn't in our interests to speak up.

Of course, I had worshipped Louis. I'd fallen in love with Gaby Hoffmann and Amy Landecker watching them on his show. A lot of what happened in my early years of becoming a director was powered by a wild jealousy of Louis C.K. and Lena Dunham. What they were doing filmically and tonally was something I felt I should know how to do. They had this kind of artistic *lack* of pushing, a slow, relaxed centering of their own shame. Looking at my work next to theirs, suddenly all of the pilot scripts I'd ever written for TV seemed to be coated in a candy shell of fakeness, a polite and pretty defense that obscured what was human and nuanced, and, therefore, true and funny.

When *Transparent* started getting nominated for awards I would run into Louis at events and my heart would thump a little. *This is crazy,* I would think. *Everything I've ever wanted has happened professionally, and yet I'm still scared to talk to him. Why do I need approval from this red-haired Daddy golem?*

You are colleagues now, I reminded myself at a party one night. We were in a courtyard between two skyscrapers. There was a bright red AstroTurf carpet with everyone famous you've ever wanted to see in one place and dessert in tiny plastic goblets with little wooden spoons. "I'm going to go up to him," I whispered to a friend. Louis smiled as someone introduced us.

"I've heard great things about your show," he said, "but I haven't seen it."

"Aw, it's cool, no one has time."

Maybe we made small talk, or maybe he quickly turned to another person. I was a lesbian at this point anyway, so I didn't expect him to flirt or light up for me—or maybe I did. After all, there were all the days of my cute and youthful glory when I would have gotten overflowing attention from a hero like him even if I had no TV show or success at all. With rare exception, men like Louis generally do that toe-to-toe comedy sparring thing only with men they admire, and there was no space for me socially as a person who was more or less at his same professional stature.

In her book *A Woman Looking at Men Looking at Women*, Siri Hustvedt suggests that a lively intellectual combat in the spirit of friendly competition is what drives most men. Many cis men are actually doing this all day at work, this emotional choreography of attempting to dunk on one another. But Hustvedt says that an intellectual or professional win against a woman in front of another man simply doesn't carry enough points to be a real win, so men don't bother engaging in this way.

This means that the potential mentorship that comes from admiration, or a random joyful social moment where someone might say *Hey, I had a good time talking to that dude at the party, let me see if he wants to come work on the show* isn't an option for many women, queer folk, or people of color. Massive opportunities like this are casually given to white cis men. There was never one black writer for all those decades on *David Letterman*. Marc Maron said he simply never hired a woman as a writer because he just felt more comfortable in a group of men.

The ways women had been kept from power, intentionally and accidentally, were more and more obvious. We added up every imagined slight and lost opportunity. There was a rush of new ideas everywhere I turned. Every day another article or two about consent was coming out. I inhaled the morning news each day. I went out for my morning walk and climbed the hills of Griffith Park, my chest filling with possibility. Fuck yes, it was all coming down. The world was realizing things.

The corroboration, conscious and unconscious, from men. We were victimized on a massive scale, we realized, but we also witnessed the deep history of how men had been backing up one another's lies, protecting not only reputations but also personal assets by spending company money secretly on nondisclosure agreements. I burned at the thought of male producers giving men money to write screenplays and then giving other men money to direct them, but never buying women's stories or hiring them to make film or television. And then these same men sitting in rooms with lawyers to read aloud private statements about a woman someone worked with and then fucked. Gretchen Carlson got paid over $20 million to keep quiet about Bill O'Reilly. She got more money to *not* say what happened to her than any woman has ever been given to tell her life story.

Can anyone calculate the dollar amount that has been spent to put duct tape over women's mouths in comparison to the amount these companies have paid women to write or direct? I want to compare the money spent on quieting every unspoken truth against every unsold screenplay, unpublished article, and rejected application. I thought of all the broke women trying to hack it, and all the men in business suits with stacks of cash, handing money over only in exchange for silence instead of art. My heart thumped with the dream of demanding transparency, forcing all companies to reveal how much they had paid women to be silent. We had been so unprotected.

In the first few weeks of this toppling, women began gathering everywhere to hatch plans. I got an email from Reese Witherspoon, inviting me to a meeting with a bunch of other women at Creative Artists Agency. I'd met Reese a few times at social gatherings and we'd almost made a few projects together. No one was quite sure what we were going to do, but we all knew we were going to do something. She hooked me up with a woman at CAA named Maha Dakhil. Maha and I wrote back and forth a few times. Can I bring a few people? I asked. Sure, she said. I emailed the queer people within easy reach, my partner at Topple, Andrea Sperling, and my friends/rabble-rousers/revolutionaries Angela Robinson and Alex Kondracke. If the door was going to open, I was going to bring a few queer women of color with me.

Later that day, I drove to the massive Death Star of a building that houses CAA. My agency, UTA, is also large, but it's homey and artsy compared to this hulking thing clad in metal slats, a powerful, foreboding edifice. I gave my car keys to the parking attendant and walked into the enormous lobby, twisting the sweaty valet ticket in my pocket. That huge lobby opened onto another huge lobby. I was about to come face-to-face with mega-power. I went to the desk.

"I'm here for the . . . uh—women's meeting?"

"Sure, your name?"

"Uh, Jill Soloway?"

"Sure, go ahead and sit down over there, someone will be down to get you."

A sensationally dressed young assistant came to get me and led me into an elevator. I went up to the seventh floor and into a conference room. Women were sitting around a huge table. There were names on cards. How did I get here? Was that my name on a card, too? There was Reese Witherspoon and America Ferrera, Ava DuVernay, and Shonda Rhimes. Natalie Portman and Rashida Jones. Super-producers like Kathleen Kennedy and Amy Pascal. Feminist political heroes like Nina Shaw and Tina Tchen. Executives I'd known. People I'd come across, acquaintances and friends, amazing people from here and there. All of us. In one room. Deciding what we were going to do. Then Oprah came in. We could do anything.

A couple weeks later there was another meeting. Everything got more intense. More people came, including data scientists and a badass researcher named Stacy Smith. Obama's chief technology officer Megan Smith. People from Women in Film and Sundance. We put Post-it notes on the board listing our goals. Where are the biggest problems? What was the difference between an NDA and a settlement agreement? "Unlock all NDAs," I wrote on a Post-it, having no idea what that really meant. I scribbled furious notes. Were we going to make demands? What about pledges? Could we get people to diversify their boards? What could we ask for? "Fifty-fifty by 2525," someone said. "Fifty-fifty by 2020," someone else said. What did "fifty-fifty" mean?

How can we be sure people of color, queer people, and the disability community are represented as we demand access? What would it mean for us to be intersectional? I found myself saying that we couldn't move forward unless we had a real plan for inclusion. Could an intersectional power movement actually happen with this much cultural power? What would we name this group? Katie McGrath said "Time's Up," and the name stuck.

That night I went home overflowing. The revolution was happening.

I was elated the next morning as I drove to work. The Topple offices on the Paramount lot felt more light filled than ever. I loved the triple-high ceilings—the weathered loft used to be a workspace for painting giant backdrops, and it was a beautiful, airy place to work. I dashed into Andrea's office and we huddled in a postgame strategy about the Time's Up meetings at CAA. There was so much to do, but first we were going to the writers' building to see how the story for Season Five of *Transparent* was going.

After the fourth season, a few of our original writers had moved on to other shows and their own overall deals. We had a fantastic new writers' room, led by a veteran showrunner named Jill Gordon. We had some new baby writers, two of whom were trans women. The room was more queer than ever. Three trans women, two nonbinary-ish folks, and Gabe, someone we jokingly referred to as the Last Remaining Cis Man.

Faith intercepted us before we got to the room. "Have you seen Van's Facebook?" she asked.

"No, what's up?"

I pulled out my phone and scrolled to Van's home page.

She hadn't worked for the show for a while, and I wasn't on Facebook much so I wasn't caught up with her life. But that morning, she had written a post, full of details about years of alleged inappropriate interactions with her boss at a job she used to have. She didn't name any names. In her inimitable Ozarks style, the post ended with "Metoo? Oh YEAH, honey."

"Is she talking about Jeffrey?" I asked.

"I think so," Faith said. "Jeffrey's the only person she worked with for that long."

I turned to Andrea. What should we do? We checked with more people who worked on the show who knew Van. The specifics of the ensuing weeks are subject to various legal restrictions and privacy considerations, but Andrea and I spoke with as many people as possible in an effort to understand the difference between inappropriate and unprofessional behavior, sexual harassment, and sexual discrimination. What constituted a serious offense when quite a few folks on the show occasionally made inappropriate jokes? This was the culture of every TV show I'd ever worked on. I'd always assumed that some people were more sensitive to that atmosphere than others and prided myself on my genderless ability to push past the dudes' edges when it came to humor. *This was about humor, right?*

I wanted so badly for it all to be a big misunderstanding. A few days earlier I'd scrawled "Unlock all NDAs" on a Post-it at CAA, and now I was wondering if there was an amount of money that could put an end to all of this before it got out of hand.

As we waited to hear back from Amazon about legal procedures and next steps, Andrea and I struggled with various feminist, psychological, and professional knots, trying to wriggle our way out of the puzzle. We had created a show highlighting trans women's voices, and Van voicing her story might end the show. Everyone's livelihood. This cultural legacy. The irony was a knot that wouldn't untie easily.

A few nights later I was at a fundraiser for St. John's, an organization that supports trans health care. It was a night of drag and trans performance, with Laverne Cox taking the stage and JD Samson deejaying. It seemed like every trans and gender-nonconforming person in L.A. was there, including a lot of people who had worked on the show over the years.

There was an auction. Should I bid? I wondered. I never know how to act in those situations. Over the years I'd watched Hollywood's power people wave their hands in the air during auctions. *Maybe I should contribute,* I thought, *or maybe that would be showing off?* I still didn't have a real bead on whether I was an insider or an outsider at these events. I had come out here and there in articles as nonbinary, but that didn't mean I could stand under the transbrella and claim this community or the word "trans" as mine. As I contemplated how to fit in but not disappear, I saw Van across the room.

It was a surprise to see her in L.A. As far as anyone knew, she had moved back to Missouri and was living outside of St. Louis. I waved and walked over. It was too loud to talk so we went outside and stood in front of the club. The ground was wet; it had just rained. The colors of neon signs bled across the puddles. Van called me Daddy, which a lot of trans women did, just to be sweet. As awkward as it felt to be somewhere between trans and cis, I could always depend on most trans women to be playful and kind about getting my gender right. That's one of the nice social currencies trans folk offer one another: Let me know the gender you want to be and I will treat you like that.

"You look good; you should start thinking about going on T," she said.

"Really?" I asked. "I wonder what that would be like, a low dose of testosterone. Are there nonbinary doses of T?"

"Yes, for sure, there have to be," she said. "I think I've heard about that."

"Maybe I'll check with my doctor," I said.

I paused.

Finally, I said, "So I heard about the Facebook post."

"Yeah," she said.

"What do you want to do about it?" I asked.

"I'm not sure," she said.

"I've been learning a lot lately," I said. "I'll send you the link to the Equal Employment Opportunity Commission's definition of what's considered against the law."

"Great," she said. "I'm going back to St. Louis, but let's talk. You should talk to some other people, too."

We hugged goodbye. The next day I sent Van the link to the EEOC page. The language said that petty slights and annoyances are not illegal. But how would anyone know the difference between petty slights and annoyances and unlawful behavior?

I felt myself splitting in two. On the outside, I was part of a cultural explosion. On the inside, I hated myself for questioning the legitimacy of Van's claims. Yes, believe all victims but—damn it—how could this happen on my show, too?

There was a push to find an outside investigator. Sexual harassment specialists were in the midst of a gold rush. It was like florists having a few hundred Valentine's Days suddenly heaped upon them in one week. Hopefully this investigation would happen quickly enough that we could steady the ship.

A few days later I got a call. A journalist had found Van's Facebook post and it was about to go public. I had thought we were dealing only with Van and her few hundred followers. Suddenly *Deadline*, *The Hollywood Reporter*, and *Variety* were emailing me: Do you have a comment on Van's Facebook post?

Everyone flew into a panic. No one could say anything publicly because the investigation hadn't yet started. Jeffrey fired off a public response that Van was disgruntled, and that her accusations were false. We tried to get him to apologize, hoping he could understand that he, and our show, were newly welcomed guests within a vulnerable community, but he was already pulling up stakes, in self-protection mode.

And what were we going to do about the show?

I didn't know.

We had already broken an entire story line with the family up to their usual hijinks. We couldn't make a move, publicly or privately, so we had to keep multiple versions of reality going in the writers' room. We started working on a version where Maura died. I kept trying to imagine a third path, just like I'd tried to do with our Israel compromise.

One morning I went to work for a meeting with the writer Malcolm Spellman about an adaptation of Marlon James's book *A Brief History of Seven Killings* that we were producing. Andrea grabbed me before I could get into the conference room.

"Trace went to *The Hollywood Reporter*," she said. "She's coming out against Jeffrey, too."

Holy fuck.

If Trace released a statement, it would be over for Jeffrey. And that meant Maura. The show. Our TV family. Everything.

"What does she say in it?"

"No one knows," Andrea said, "but they may send it to us before it gets published."

I went into the meeting with Malcolm, trying not to get distracted by possible multiple realities. I figured Trace's statement was going to be about the aspects of Jeffrey's personality that all of us knew—how he sometimes bullied people, had a bad temper, and that women had absolutely received more of this than men.

But when the *Reporter* sent us an advance copy of her letter, asking for our comment, it was more damning. She named a specific time that he'd said he wanted to "attack her sexually" and later pressed his groin against her.

Holy fucking shit.

I had to talk to Trace.

I texted her: "Can we talk?"

"Actually, I happen to be on the lot," she said. "I have a meeting. I'll be done in an hour."

"Great," I said. "Let's meet at the Coffee Bean."

My heart pounded. I needed to find out why she was

going straight to the press with her story, to understand why she hadn't come to us. We could handle this, I wanted to tell her, but let us do it internally, inside the family.

I hyperventilated as I waited for the meeting, then went to the Coffee Bean.

When I got there, we sat down at some picnic tables. I could see the whole future of the show, everything I had worked for, all of it spinning out.

"I can't believe you're doing this," I said.

"Well, it happened to me," she said.

"But why didn't you come to us?"

"Why didn't you come to me?" she asked.

"How could I have come to you?" I said. "I didn't even know it happened. This was three years ago."

"Van told me she told you to talk to me."

I thought back in my mind. Did Van tell me to talk to Trace that night outside of the St. John's benefit? She had told me I should talk to other people, and I had given all of the names of anyone I thought might be able to shed light on the inquiry to the investigator, including Trace's. Maybe they hadn't called her yet. Maybe things weren't happening fast enough.

"I had to tell my story," she said. "But I said in my statement that I wanted the show to continue."

"But the idea of the show will be tarnished now in everyone's minds," I said. "In Middle America when people think of trans people there's still so much suspicion, and Maura became this beautiful symbol of transness and now you're laying this imagery out there of her being a predator."

Suddenly, I started crying.

She was horrified.

"I'm the victim here and YOU'RE crying?" she demanded.

She was right. I was sitting across from her, frozen with fear. I tried to stop myself from crying. Like Michael in *The Godfather*, I tried to play it stoic and cool. I didn't say, *Fredo, after all I've done for you.* I said, "I wish you luck."

And then I walked away.

An hour later the article came out.

15   THE VULNERABLE FUTURE

TRACE'S STORY WAS PICKED UP EVERYWHERE. SOON AFTER, I WAS on my morning hike when I saw my neighbor Mary walking her sheepdog.

"So, did he *do* it?" she asked.

"Did *who* do *what*?" I said quietly.

"Your show. That guy. Did he do it?"

"We don't know yet," I answered, and went on my way.

I couldn't believe what had happened to our beautiful show, my legacy, the thing that felt like the most important thing I'd ever done.

Yet I had to remind myself that it wasn't Van's or Trace's fault for being willing to speak. This happened because of Jeffrey and how his male privilege, his place in the patriarchy, blinded him to how his actions affected others.

When something bad is happening, my first impulse is to look away. If I hear a noise in bed, I'll put my pillow over my head and spend five full minutes listening to a distant animal in pain or helicopters over the neighbor's yard before I trust I'm actually hearing it.

I wanted so badly to make everything that was happening go away. To disappear it.

FOLKS IN THE cast and on the crew couldn't be there for one another during the investigation. I wasn't allowed to communicate with Trace. I knew she must have felt horrible after our conversation.

We did crisis management with the cast, the crew, the writers. Conversations. Circles. Hikes. More reporters hounded more people for more details. Writers got random emails from journalists. There were real leaks and imaginary leaks everywhere. Who is talking to the press? Who is keeping things in the family? PR folks kept gossip columnists away from the actors. *Does anyone know if he did it? Whatever it is?*

Amid all of the maybes, I kept wondering what would have happened if I'd been able to get Jeffrey to apologize to Van rather than accuse her of lying. I'd heard from friends that Jeffrey was insisting he'd always engaged in a consensual and playful dynamic. He said he was flirtatious and bawdy, and claimed that it was, in fact, a beloved part of working on a show about sex and boundaries. I heard from others that he was considering dropping the bombshell to a journalist that *Transparent* was the most sex-obsessed set he'd ever been on. But in his own self-assessment, Jeffrey separated the culture of occasional sex jokes from his anger and displays of immense moodiness. His rages. His power. He didn't see how, when layered together, he became someone who some people were afraid of.

Jeffrey thought that trans women were holding on to a righteous anger at the show, at cis people defining reality for trans folk. And I knew that cis women know how this feels, how it feels for men to not see them as people. To see them as something Other instead.

And what does it mean that only trans women accused him? Zackary Drucker once told me that when she discloses her transness to a cis man, if they are alone, that man will turn the conversation sexual almost 100 percent of the time. I find that happens sometimes when I come out to a straight man in a casual conversation about being nonbinary or even queer—they start talking to me about sex.

OUT IN THE MEDIA, I was noticing that *She misunderstood my actions* was the best men could come up with, short of apologies. The same arguments were coming up whether people were talking about a dirty joke or a date or sex or rape. Men thought one thing was happening, and women thought another.

For most people, the masculine yes means Go Toward It, and the feminine yes is known for what it holds or takes in. It means *come in,* assuming default hetero cis bodies anyway. If you look at these two shapes, they deepen when in relationship to patriarchy. Meaningful consent becomes a setup for a clash. Multiple versions of reality. Men have more power than they ever consciously realize and women have less than they ever imagine. A lot of people, especially women living in patriarchy, may end up saying yes even when they don't want to. Maybe they're afraid they may not be heard, or maybe they say yes when they want to say no because the times in the past where they have said no and not been heard were so traumatizing that they think if they say yes *this time,* they can gain control over the pain of the previous experience.

I don't want it is also something people of color, queer people, disabled people, or other otherized people can rarely say aloud safely at work.

The structure of patriarchy offers assistance to a male-created reality. Jeffrey's power on the set, plus his temper and his sexual suggestiveness, when combined with the institutional power of patriarchy, made his interactions different from other people's. Was it my job to help him understand this?

THERE'S A HUGE problem with the way the law treats consent like a snapshot, as if it happens only in one particular moment. But it doesn't. You can say yes to a compliment about your clothes and no to a recounting of a sex dream someone had about you. You can say yes to kissing and no to intercourse. Yes to vaginal and no to anal. True consent is an ongoing ethical conversation that lasts for hours or days or months or years.

What's problematic is that amid so much confusion around consent, we continue to collectively reinforce the idea that when sex is present, power is also present. *Cosmo* encourages us to play sex games. *You be the teacher, I'll be the student. You be the boss, I'll be the secretary.* We all agree this is fun and we like it. But bosses don't really tell their secretaries to take their tops off. Consent means one partner saying to another: *Let's agree to play boss and secretary.*

When a man finds himself at the breakfast table reading another *New York Times* article about what he sees as fuzzy consent, and then debates with his wife about whether or not someone actually "wanted it," I wonder if these confused men are subconsciously fighting for the right to be *turned on* by the boundaryless movement from no to yes. *This is a staple of seduction, right?* they may wonder. As the one who goes in, maybe they light up to the idea that women are somehow essentially different, and this is how it would feel to go from no to yes. It would be fun, right?

The discrepancy between the mouth and the pussy is a subject that has kept men busy talking about consent for years. That you might want it, but you don't know this until they tell you. And what about when women *do* want it? The current explosion is about what gets done to women who say no, or who think no. What about the women who wanted it? But maybe only wanted *part* of what *it* even is? We don't only want freedom from other people's unwanted desire, we also need total freedom *to* desire.

I imagine women running free. Owning the world and being loose and wild. And then I think about the artist Louise Bourgeois's drawing *Sainte Sébastienne,* sometimes called *The Arrows of Stress.* About the series of drawings she did on this subject, Bourgeois said, "She becomes frightened for what she is responsible for. . . . She was not prepared. . . . She is very vulnerable. This is a self-portrait of a person who is very happy and running and then suddenly realizes she has antagonized people. She gets shot at."

Who would we be if we weren't afraid of what our state of wanting might incite? Not just wanting to be free from male desire, but free to explore our own? Free to want?

———

MORE AND MORE men kept going down. All of these men putting women in positions of discomfort and then watching what happened. I wondered if a certain generation of men would cheerily agree that *all* of men's interactions with women were a slow gaining of consent. Are women slightly more talented at reinventing their own bodily realities to just *get into it*? How many times did I do that?

Men don't realize the rage underneath our realizations that we were fucked up by Bruce Springsteen singing, *Hey, little girl, is your daddy home . . . oh oh oh, I'm on fire,* or Rod Stewart telling me that tonight was the night and he was going to spread my wings so he could come inside. We all sang along.

Men also don't realize what it feels like to realize we were raised knowing that we will have to allow access to our bodies when we grow up. One day something will go in there. One day you will put a tampon in there, or a penis in there, one day you will go to the doctor and he will open your legs and look in there, get ready. Men have been helpfully trying to let us know that something will go in, and that we need to be okay with it. There will be access. There will be blood. You will be opened. I have always been so angry about this. How they have made it their job to tell us about how this will go.

If all men are guilty, which ones are going down and why? Would all of this be solved if we had two different ways of saying yes? One that means *I'm going toward that* and one that means *Come on in*? Do we need a truth and reconciliation committee like they had in South Africa?

Maybe this is what Time's Up could be. One at a time, men go into a room with all of the women, or whoever can make it that day. What did you do? Did you take access because you thought you could? This is your penance.

THE *TRANSPARENT* WRITERS and staff and actors waited for a couple of excruciating months, and then one day got the call. The investigation had been concluded. A decision had been made.

They wanted us to move forward without Jeffrey.

I don't know why I had thought somehow we would find a third way. Like thinking magic would save my marriage. But there wasn't any magic to be found. Our start date was pushed. The crew was told to dismantle the Pfefferman house set we'd been building at Paramount.

Coming up with the new season had been impossible in the face of all of the not knowing. At every juncture, I kept wanting to tell Andrea and the folks at Amazon that the writers' room was pumping away, amid the drama. We would figure this one out.

But I was lying. Post reckoning, everyone was writing, but none of the beauty or joy was there. Before the reckoning our creativity was like a popcorn machine, overflowing everywhere. All we had to do was scoop up the popcorn.

The folks at Amazon were unsure if there was a version of the show we could all still imagine. I wanted to imagine it. I kept feeling around for inspiration. What is still alive? But as the accusations flooded social media, I felt someone wagging a finger at me: *Look, it all came tumbling down.* We started to lose crew members. Jimmy Frohna took a job as the cinematographer on *Big Little Lies* and Andrea Arnold was going to be the director and executive producer. I felt more pangs of loss. Not that I would have stopped Jimmy from taking the job, but of course I felt possessive of him. His crew. Our gaffer and key grip, plus our assistant directors, also joined that show.

Trace kept saying to the press that she wanted the show to return, but it wasn't that easy. I used to talk about how the show wrote itself. The show was writing itself because we existed in a bubble of trust and co-conspiratorial force. Could anything still work without the trust? Whatever was organic and part of the soil, it couldn't just be snapped back into reality. We would have to rebuild.

It suddenly all felt so vulnerable. Our show wasn't just a place where a cis man played a trans woman. It was the only show that had ever existed that succeeded by diving deeply into what library nerds call the HQ70s, a place that holds the books about queer Jews, Magnus Hirschfeld and Sarah Schulman and Leslie Feinberg. I felt defensive of our category. Was it all over?

A MONTH OR so later, I went to see Ellen. We were still in a holding pattern with the show, and she was very much alive and thriving—a black eye on the face of all pancreatic cancer research and death stats that had come before.

As I sat down she said, "Guess what my housekeeper said when you came in?"

"What?" I asked.

" 'He's here.' "

Ha, we both laughed.

I told her that I was leaving the next day for New York. It was Faith's birthday and Felix's spring break and also Passover. Faith and some super powerful Broadway singers we'd found would be premiering *Faith Soloway and Friends*. She was showcasing all of the songs she'd been writing over the years for an imaginary *Transparent* musical. When our parent had first come out, Faith and I had responded by deciding we were going to make a documentary musical. We filmed a little of it the first time we saw Carrie as herself.

Faith can write songs about anything and everything with zero notice. She plays by ear and the melodies are beautiful and the lyrics are astonishing. Before she came to work on *Transparent,* she had been mounting rock operas in Boston, folk songs, light operas, and sweet arias. But she only ever performed her shows for one or two nights, never really wanting to deal with the admin of producing a run.

Now, five years later, she had a stack of songs about our family and the Pfeffermans. She had also been writing songs about gender long before our parent came out, with names like "NeverGenderland," an absurd *Fantasia*-inspired amusement park you could visit where you could be anyone you needed to be.

"That sounds amazing," Ellen said. "I wish I could come see it."

"What does it mean that the thing I love the most is making things? The only way I can deal with all this trauma is to get lost in the next thing."

"You need to teach yourself how to be," she said.

"Agreed," I said.

"You think you have to say it out loud for it to be true."

"Say what out loud?" I asked.

"Who you want to be."

"Oh," I lied, like I got it.

"You don't have to say anything out loud," she said. "Just find a time when you're supposed to feel joy. Then just say it to yourself over and over again: JOY. JOY. JOY."

Was she saying that all I should do was just stop worrying and have the people I love over as much as I can and have great food? Get the standing order, bagels and a spread, on Sundays and gather, just like we learned from reality TV. Maybe watching our own TV show about our family could help us learn who we wanted our family to become.

IN NEW YORK, I walked past the spot where twenty-five years before, Faith and I had opened *The Real Live Brady Bunch* play at the now-long-gone Village Gate. It had originated at the Annoyance Theatre in Chicago, where it had been a huge success, and then within a year suffered a violent political split into Those Going to New York on the *Brady Gravy Train* and Those Staying Behind in Chicago to Take a Stand for Real Theater.

Half of us huffed off and moved out, fifty or so of us converging on the square mile surrounding Fourteenth and Hudson carrying luggage in giant laundry bags. Twenty people lived in one loft together. Some made rooms out of blankets. I lived in the third floor of a townhouse with Faith and our friend Eric and my boyfriend Peter. We walked down Bleecker every night to our shows at the Village Gate; door-to-door was thirteen minutes from Bethune. We drank Hefeweizen with lemon at the White Horse Tavern. It was overwhelming and we felt free and even a little famous. Minute to minute livin' it, amid the vibrating carpet of connection we used to create when we didn't have cellphones yet.

That theater company is still thriving, even though at the explosion moment it seemed like only one side would survive. Everyone re-formed into new groups. Maybe it's just a science thing, ecosystems not being able to hold more than a hundred people, organisms splitting like embryos twinning. The constant of evolution and transformation.

The city felt so familiar now, walking these streets again with Isaac and Felix. Isaac is a junior in college and Felix is in third grade. Bruce has a new girlfriend; he is in love. We don't take turns every few hours now; we do it every week or so. So much has changed. It's weird that so much feels the same.

I AM STILL compelled by the idea that I have to hurry and change the world before I die. That feeling of being chased is always here. Post reckoning, what am *I* doing to get what I want? What am I doing to topple the patriarchy? It never feels like enough. While I was in New York I went to speak to a room full of funders about 5050by2020, our emergent activist arm of Time's Up. Stumping for whatever this new idea is, this word we haven't invented yet, this less gooey version of "melting pot," some other word that means powerful solidarity around understanding intersectionality and inclusion. Maybe the right word is "pluralism." To get inside of the messiness of our interconnected otherness. Putting ourselves in those spaces *is* the revolution. Amid these clashes, we are forced to dance around our own binaries to pass particular tests about where some are and aren't welcome. We are all way far gone, way beyond meshed up inside our ways of being Other. No one can choose between Jew or Queer or Cis or Trans or Woman. It's too late. Our roots have formed webs, the way all the trees talk to one another, always connecting up underground. It's all one thing.

I am wishing for a massive transbrella army, the bigger the better, all people who feel androgynous, including those who occasionally like to upend people's gender expectations, plus, of course, trans folk and intersex people and drag queens. We could all be one gigantic designation of those who check X on their driver's licenses—a delegation of the third box, the non-box, not even a thing that goes in the box and also the box. Power to the people, or at least those children of the box, those who grab on to hold one another's hands to cross the busy intersection.

ONE NIGHT AFTER we all went out for Faith's birthday dinner, she and I walked back to our hotel. We were both sad that Moppa couldn't join us. Her foot had been hurting and she wanted to rest.

We talked about this book. That it was almost done.

"Are you still planning on calling it *She Wants It*?" Faith asked.

"Yeah," I said.

We walked for a little while, then I said, "You know what I never really figured out? What Carrie wanted. When we were little."

"Remember when he kept his headphones on so he could listen to the Cubs game when he came to see me in my high school orchestra recital?" Faith asked.

"Do you think he wanted to listen to the Cubs game during your recital because he was anxious about moving through the world in a gender fugue and listening to the Cubs game was the only way he could calm down?" I posited.

"No," she said. "I think he just wanted to listen to the Cubs game."

"Or did he want to stand out in the crowd of parents who had all come with genuine admiration for their children?" I asked. "Did he need to be different, the one person who wasn't actually listening? Did he need to be exhibitionistic about his difference? Was he trying to be silly, trying to get attention for his absurdism?"

"I think he just wanted to listen to the Cubs game."

Maybe sometimes as parents we're just trying to feel okay, and maybe sometimes that means having a barrier between ourselves and the rest of the world.

Ellen recently told me, "You can let people hold you, you know." As adults we give up on that ask, to lie like a baby in someone's arms, or we give up on that offer, *C'mere, I made this space for you, come in.*

In our family there was a lot of space for joy, too. Our bird calls, the funny Britishisms that Carrie brought from London, the nicknames and new names, the way we all knew that *klim* meant *milk*. We sang all the time. Carrie would put on WFMT on a Sunday morning and conduct the hell out of the music in our living room with an imaginary baton and wild eyes. My mom found her entertaining, hilarious. All the ways Harry wasn't a man stacked up. But now we could see why—she wasn't a man.

Carrie had such a hard time when she had to be Harry.

She told me that my grandfather raged, sometimes for days, in their childhood home. He would cut them off, abandon them over and over. What have men been raging about for all these years? What does it feel like to see your home as a place where you can be openly awful?

Is everyone just wondering, will you still love me if . . . ?

THESE DAYS I AM identifying as nonbinary because I can. Enough has accrued in an imaginary account of public goodwill that I'm not vulnerable to the kind of humiliation many could experience if they came to work and said: *FYI, I'm not a man or a woman anymore.* Or maybe I have enough power at this point, which is privilege, and I want to use my privilege for good and also to feel safe in my body. I guess, truthfully, I also want to salute and emulate the youth so that they might continue to include me in their various web arts, public gatherings, Instagram posts.

A lot of people have said to me, *Hey, Jill, rather than expand what the word "trans" means, why can't you just expand what the word "woman" means? Can't you just be this newfangled type of woman, a short-haired, non-makeup-wearing, sometimes really butch kind of a woman? If you could just call yourself that, then you would allow all women to expand their definitions of themselves and the word "woman."*

And the best answer I have is to say that it is probably *exactly that question* that makes me ultimately want to identify as trans. That question centers cis-ness, assuming it as default. It's as strange as assuming everyone would want to be male or white. I *want* to be not cis. Implicit in the question of why wouldn't

I just take the identity with more privilege misunderstands that what I prefer is the identity that feels more like home.

THE LAST TIME I visited my moppa we were in Chicago, walking past Water Tower Place, the mall I used to go to when I was a teenager.

"Jilly," they said, "you know, I don't know if I feel like a woman. I might be more like you. In between."

"That's cool, Moppa," I said. "Nobody knows anything, we're all just learning."

"Yes," they said.

Maybe they were raging way back then because nobody used "they" as a singular pronoun yet.

AND THEN LAST NIGHT we all got to the theater early and made our way to our seats. The space was a jumble of café tables and cane-back chairs and it reminded me so much of the Village Gate, those old days. That feeling of a new world unwrapping, the anticipation as the place filled up. We hobnobbed and hugged old friends. People wanted to know whether the show would be okay. Are these people still alive?

There are so many ways that Faith has come to my rescue. When we were little in South Commons, she was all tough, my protector against all bullies, those mean boys in the winter jackets with the fur around the hoods who teased me for being a crybaby.

The lights lowered and she took the stage. The band

kicked in and one by one this new family that looked a little like the Pfefferman family got in formation onstage. These amazing voices singing out the beginnings of Faith's rock opera, harmonizing through a song called "Your Boundary Is My Trigger." Another one where the kids meet Maura and ask her for one simple answer in song: "Where Have You Been?"

Faith found a woman named Shakina Nayfack to play Maura. Shakina is trans and Jewish and her name means "goddess" in Hebrew, or the "great feminine," or "she who holds space with love and patience," and I got the chills as she started singing. Like she was giving a kind of resuscitation to Maura.

I looked around at the audience. Isaac and Felix were sitting together, my mom smack dab in the center. Judith Light squeezed my arm as she watched my mom, who was bouncing in her seat cheering along as Jackie Hoffman played Shelly. Elaine sang along, loud and proud, wanting so badly to be celebrated. I wanted to hold it all, the people I loved in the audience and the ramping wild rising that was happening onstage, all of it wrapping around my heart. The music a smoke signal to ourselves and to the world that we are still alive.

What was it that Ellen said?

She said, "Remind yourself." So I did. I repeated it to myself as I sat surrounded by family, over and over again:

JOY. JOY. JOY.

Acknowledgments

WRITING THIS BOOK would not have been possible without the love and support of the many brilliant people in my life. I'm so lucky and humbled to have family, friends, collaborators, and mentors who challenge me and hold space for the ups and downs of this crazy, anxiety-provoking process.

I am indebted to my editor, Tricia Boczkowski, for holding my story in your heart and loving it as if it were your own. I am so grateful to Hilary Liftin for coming in and helping everything rise when it was falling. And to the astonishingly incisive and loving Tennessee Jones: navigating the gaze is easier said than done, but I could not have done it without you.

I am so grateful to Brett Paesel and Lori Lober, for getting deep in it with me, page by page.

Giant love and thanks to Daniel Greenberg and all the folks at Levine Greenberg Rostan.

I am so lucky that these friends read drafts and gave me their ideas and feedback, the good and the kind as well as the difficult: Tavianna Rodriguez, Jessica Yellin, Cynthia Sweeney, Carina Chocano, Iva Gueorguieva, and Sarah Schulman.

To the folks in and around Topple, both official and un-official, in my work and life work, who took on the creation of this book with me: my always partner-in-crime Andrea Sperling, Kella Birch, Genevieve Winters, Nico della Fave, Erin Kellgren, Zackary Drucker, Christina Hjelm, Megan Green, Eli Cordova, Megan Mercier, Taylor Blackburn, Rachel Ichimura, and Shay Roman.

Ellen Silverstein. Your power and wisdom transcend. I have so much love and gratitude for you and all that you are.

My team in Hollywood and beyond, all things, both business and emotional: Larry Salz, Blair Kohan, Kelly Bush, Karl Austen, Ryan LeVine, Ivy Kagan Bierman, and Howard Altman.

To my friends, mentors, and colleagues—your willing-ness to help and your brilliance astounds me: Susan Goldberg, Mel Shimkovitz, David Naggar, Jim Frohna, Mordecai Finley, Amichai Lau-Lavie, Nicole Georges, Dolly Wells, Jo Lampert, Shakina Nayfack, Alexandra Billings, Our Lady J, Kathryn Hahn, Allie Hoffman, Amanda Montell, Trace Lysette, Joe Lewis, Deanna Mustard, Kathleen Johnson, Galia Linn, Alexandra Grant, and Lauren Bon.

And whoever you are, wondering why your name isn't in here, I'm sorry, I panicked, I missed people, I realize that, will you accept my apology?

My siblings: Jen Strozier, Robin Ruzan, Carrie Aizley, and Michaela Watkins.

To Joan Scheckel for finding my purpose and giving me language and tools.

So much thanks to all of the women of Time's Up. This revolution and you inspire me. To the writers, cast, and crew of *Transparent* and *I Love Dick* for your support and love and family-making.

I love you, Eileen Myles. Thank you for your heart and for teaching me who I wanted to be.

Thank you, Lauren Cioffi, for all of the depth and joy.

I love you, Bruce. Thank you for your sensitivity and love and effortless gentle co-parenting. For letting me be me.

And to my sweet family, my children and center of my world: Felix and Isaac, Faith Soloway, Carrie Soloway, and Elaine Soloway. I know how hard it is to have someone else tell your story. I love you so much. Thanks for trusting me and loving me back.